YOUNG EUROPEAN DESIGNERS

daab

INTRODUCTION 5

5.5 Designers	12		dejanew	130
Agence A+ Créateurs D'Objects	16		Delineo Design	132
Afroditi Krassa Industrial Design Consultancy	20		Design Aid	136
			Design by us	138
Ahn and Ahn Industrial Design	24		Lilian de Souza	142
ALL+-Interieur	28		Stephanie Dietmann	144
Julian Appelius Büro für Produkt Design	32		Stefan Diez	146
Studio Claudia Santiago Areal	36		Disorder Collectiv	152
Autoban	40		element Design	156
Barber Osgerby	44		Fashionsteel Möbeldesign	160
Barney Barford	48		feinedinge handmade produktgestaltung	162
Alberto Basaglia Natalia Rota Nodari Architetti Associatii	52		Fifty-Eight b	166
Paul Bechstein	56		File studio	170
Gabriela Bellon Furniture Design	60		For Use	174
Bernstrand & Co	64		Freedom Of Creation	178
Berteling Design	68		Fremdkörper	180
Michaël Bihain Interior & Furniture design	70		Front	182
bkm Design Working Group	74		Jörg Gätjens Design Development	188
Bram Boo	78		Godart Designers	192
Todd Bracher Studio	82		Camilla Groth	194
Buro Bruno	88		gruppe RE	198
Louise Campbell	92		Doug Harper Furniture	202
chd Industrial & Product Design	96		Hippos Design Architektura	204
CIPRE Design	100		iL-studio	208
code.2.design	104		instantconcept buero für gestaltung, design, innenarchitektur	212
confused collection konzeption und gestaltung	108		irion Möbelsysteme	216
CROSS I CREATIVE Designstudios	112		Florence Jaffrain	218
daniels & koitzsch Designer	118		jehs + laub	222
Cédric Debatty	122		kafka.design	226
Maria de Ros	120		Studio Monni Karri	230
defacto.design	126		Kik!	234
			Michael Koenig	236

Lifestyle Space	240
Patrick Lindon	242
Lorenz Kaz	246
Felix Severin Mack	248
maybe design	252
Julia Maendler Designer	256
Manzlab	258
design by f maurer	262
momentum	266
monica graffeo designer	270
Roberto Monte	274
Walter Musacchi	276
Thorsten Neeland	278
Neustahl	282
Nichetto+Gai	284
Nix	290
Olze & Wilkens	292
Dieter Paul Design	296
Pearsonlloyd Design	300
Florian Petri	304
The Pfeifer Consultancy	306
Polka Product Pleasure	310
POOL22	314
jacob pringiers design studio	318
puff_buff design	322
Qubus Design Studio	326
Ransmeier&Floyd	328
Sebastian Ritzler	332
Sanniadesign	334
John Sebastian	338
speziell produktgestaltung	342
Sternform Produktgestaltung	346
Martin Struss Creative Industry	352

Studio màss	354
studio vertijet	358
Rene Sulc Industrial Design	362
Suter & Gil	366
Taione Design	370
Transalpin	374
Tibor Uhrin	378
Gary van Broekhoven	380
Wolf Udo Wagner	382
Theo Williams	386
Yunniic	390
Zampach	394
Index	396
Imprint	400

INTRODUCTION & INSPIRATION SOURCES

The increasingly faster changing trends and attitudes about life are also logically reflected in the design. In the era of mass production, media giants and a time where 'average' is expanding at an alarming rate, it is more important than ever to tackle new dimensions in design. Design does not stop at the product's wrapper, one cannot look at one's very own design work in isolation any longer, and integrated thinking is required. EU expansion is now fully underway, markets are becoming global and as a result, product and design requirements are becoming increasingly complex. On the way to a multi-cultural society, products are required that are understood beyond the cultural borders. European history as a potential for experience, in addition to recognizing current trends in society, is a further elementary part of the continuous debate on the question of what is 'young' European design is today. Who are the designers and design offices who have already made a name for themselves or who are still waiting to be discovered? What distinguishes a design from Prague with one from London, or one from Stuttgart with one from Copenhagen? What identifies or characterizes young European design? The answers are several and varying, rather than just one. Some of the works that were subjectively selected here have been awarded the highest design awards, other are still in the concept phase or are waiting for a manufacturer and marketing as prototypes. The book in question looks at what is happening in the young European design scene. As one can see, things are moving.

Die zunehmend schneller wechselnden Trends und Lebensanschauungen schlagen sich folgerichtig auch im Design nieder. Im Zeitalter der Massenprodukte, Medienriesen und des rasant ausufernden Durchschnitts ist es wichtiger den je, im Design neue Dimensionen anzugehen. Design hört nicht an der Hülle des Produktes auf, die ureigene Designarbeit kann somit nicht mehr isoliert betrachtet werden, ganzheitliches Denken ist gefragt. Inzwischen ist die EU-Erweiterung in vollem Gange, Märkte werden globaler und damit auch die Anforderungen an Produkt und Design immer komplexer. Auf dem Weg in eine multikulturelle Gesellschaft sind Produkte erforderlich, die über kulturelle Grenzen hinweg verständlich sind. Europäische Geschichte als Erfahrungspotenzial ist, neben dem Erkennen von aktuellen Strömungen in der Gesellschaft ein weiterer elementarer Teil der kontinuierlichen Auseinandersetzung bei der Frage, was ist – junges – europäisches Design heute. Welche Designer und Designbüros haben sich bereits einen Namen gemacht und welche werden erst jetzt entdeckt? Was unterscheidet Design aus Prag von dem aus London, dem aus Stuttgart mit dem aus Kopenhagen? Was kennzeichnet, was zeichnet junges europäisches Design aus? Eine Antwort wird es kaum geben, eher mehrere und unterschiedliche. Einige der hier subjektiv ausgewählten Arbeiten sind mit höchsten Designpreisen ausgezeichnet, andere befinden sich noch in der Konzeptphase oder warten als Prototypen auf einen Hersteller und Vertrieb. Das vorliegende Buch gibt einen Überblick über das Geschehen in der jungen europäischen Designszene. Wie man sieht, ist einiges in Bewegung.

Les modes et notre vision du monde changent de plus en plus vite, ce qui en toute logique affecte aussi le monde du design. A l'époque de la consommation de masse, des géants des médias et de la médiocrité galopante, il est plus important que jamais de concéder au design la place qui lui revient. Le design ne se limite pas à l'emballage du produit, le travail personnel du designer ne peut plus être envisagé de manière isolée, une vision globale des choses s'impose. De plus l'élargissement de l'UE est en cours, les marchés se globalisent et les exigences concernant les produits et le design deviennent de plus en plus complexes. Sur la voie d'une société multiculturelle, il est nécessaire d'avoir des produits qui sont commercialisables dans des pays de cultures différentes. Parallèlement à l'identification des courants actuels au sein de la société, la perception de l'Histoire européenne en tant que potentiel d'expérimentation représente un élément essentiel du débat sans fin sur la définition du jeune design européen d'aujourd'hui. Quels designers et quels bureaux de design ont déjà un nom et lesquels sont en train de s'en faire un ? Quels sont les éléments qui différencient le design de Prague de celui de Londres, celui de Stuttgart de celui de Copenhague ? Quelles sont les caractéristiques, les particularités du Jeune Design Européen ? Il n'existe pas une mais plusieurs réponses, toutes différentes, à ces questions. Quelques uns des travaux sélectionnés dans cet ouvrage ont reçu les prix Design les plus convoités, d'autres sont encore en phase de conception ou à l'état de prototypes en attente d'un producteur et de leur commercialisation. Ce livre donne un aperçu des évènements de la scène du Jeune Design Européen. Comme vous pouvez le constater, le monde bouge.

El rápido incremento de las tendencias cambiantes y formas de encarar la vida también precipitan sus consecuencias en el diseño. En la era de los productos de consumo masivo, gigantes de medios de comunicación y rasante desborde del promedio, es más importante que nunca, encarar nuevas dimensiones en el diseño. El diseño no termina en la envoltura del producto, el trabajo de diseño original de esta manera no puede ser más considerado de forma aislada, se solicita un pensamiento integral. Entretanto la ampliación de la UE se encuentra en plena marcha, los mercados se tornan más globalizados y con ello también los requerimientos al producto y diseño se tornan cada vez más complejos. En la ruta hacia una sociedad multicultural se requieren productos, que sean comprensibles más allá de los límites culturales. La historia de Europa como potencial de experiencia es, junto con el reconocimiento de las actuales corrientes en la sociedad, un otro componente elemental de la continua discusión sobre la pregunta, que es diseño – joven – europeo. ¿Que diseñadores y estudios de diseño se han hecho ya de un nombre y cuales recién ahora son descubiertos? ¿Que diferencia un diseñador de Praga de uno dé Londres, el de Stuttgart con uno de Copenhague? ¿Que caracteriza, que distingue al diseño joven europeo? Una sola respuesta apenas se podrá obtener, más bien varias y diferentes. Algunos de los trabajos aquí subjetivamente seleccionados han sido galardonados con los máximos premios de diseño, otros se encuentran aún en fase de concepto o aguardan como prototipos a un fabricante y comercialización. El presente libro le ofrece una visión sobre los sucesos en la escena del diseño joven europeo. Como puede verse, algo se está moviendo.

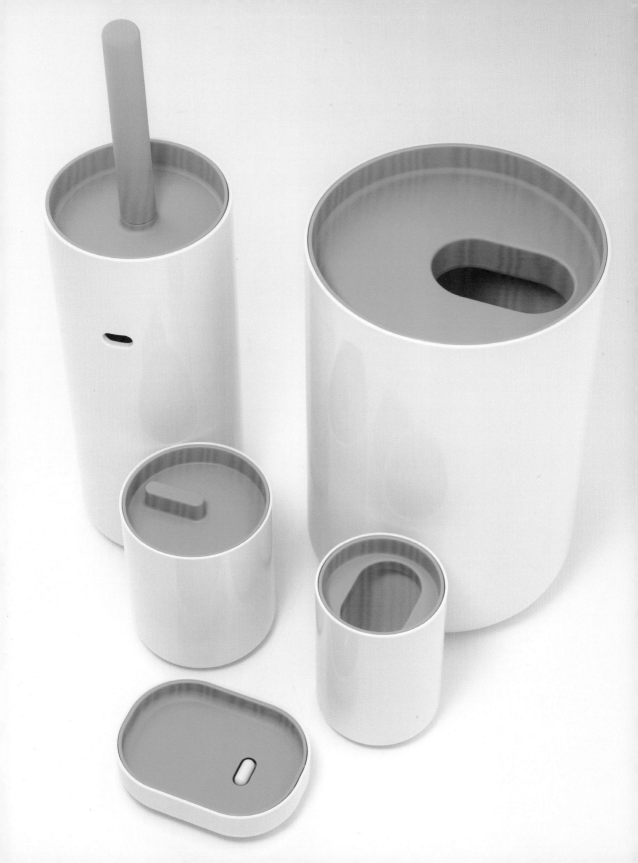

I trend e le visioni della vita che mutano con rapidità, in misura sempre crescente riguardano conseguentemente anche il design. Nell'era dei prodotti di massa, dei colossi dell'informazione e della media che degenera a velocità vertiginosa, è più importante affrontare di volta in volta le nuove dimensioni del design. Il design non termina con l'involucro del prodotto, il lavoro di design personale, quindi, non può essere più considerato in modo esclusivo, ma è richiesto un concetto globale. Nel frattempo, l'espansione della UE è in pieno progresso, i mercati diventano più globali e, quindi, anche i requisiti del prodotto e del design sempre più complessi. Sulla strada che porta a una società multiculturale è necessario che i prodotti siano comprensibili aldilà delle frontiere culturali. La storia europea, come potenziale di esperienze, oltre all'identificazione dei flussi attuali nella società, è un'ulteriore particella elementare della discussione continua relativa alla domanda su cosa sia al giorno d'oggi il design europeo moderno. Quali designer e studi di design si sono già fatti un nome e quali sono stati scoperti solo ora? Cosa differenzia il design di Praga da quello di Londra, da quello di Stoccarda con quello di Copenhagen? Cosa caratterizza e contraddistingue il design europeo moderno? Non è possibile dare una risposta univoca, ma tante e di tipo diverso. Alcuni dei lavori, qui selezionati in modo soggettivo, sono stati premiati nei concorsi di design più prestigiosi, altri sono ancora nella fase concettuale o attendono come prototipi un produttore e un distributore. Il presente libro fornisce una panoramica sugli avvenimenti della moderna scena del design europeo. Come si vede, qualcosa si muove.

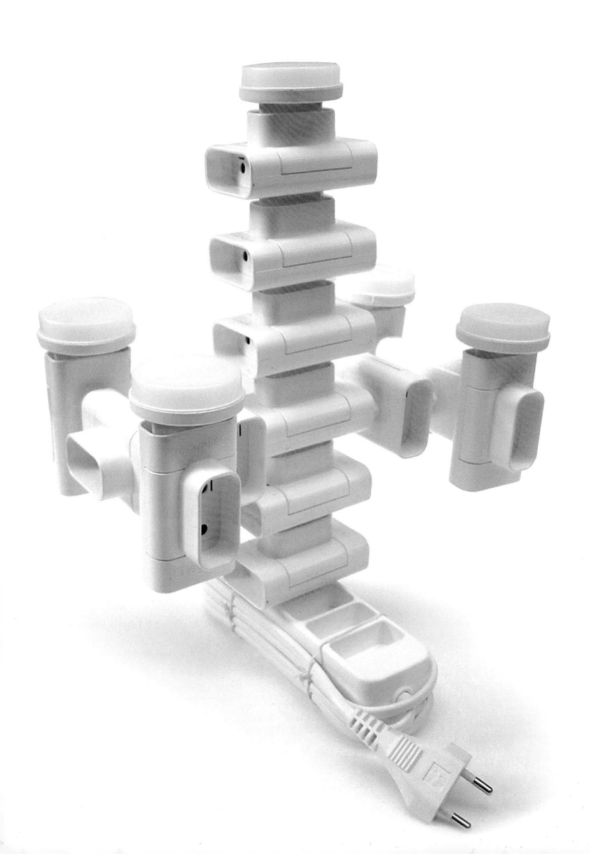

5.5 DESIGNERS | PARIS, FRANCE

Anthony Lebossé, Claire Renard, David Lebreton,
J. Sébastian Blanc, Vincent Baranger

5.5 Designers specialize in new interpretations of existing products. They take the everyday and make it fascinating.

www.cinqcinqdesigners.com

1 Chandelier 3000
2 Presse citron de star
3 Anse de sucre
4 Pied de Verre
5 Porte Cindre
6 Lampe Branchée

2

3

4

5

AGENCE A+ CRÉATEURS D'OBJECTS | PARIS, FRANCE
Arno

As a designer, Arno cannot be categorized in one specific area. With his products, he offers simple solutions for everyday problems.

www.a-plus.fr

1 Alum
2 Six
3 Tangram
4 Carafe

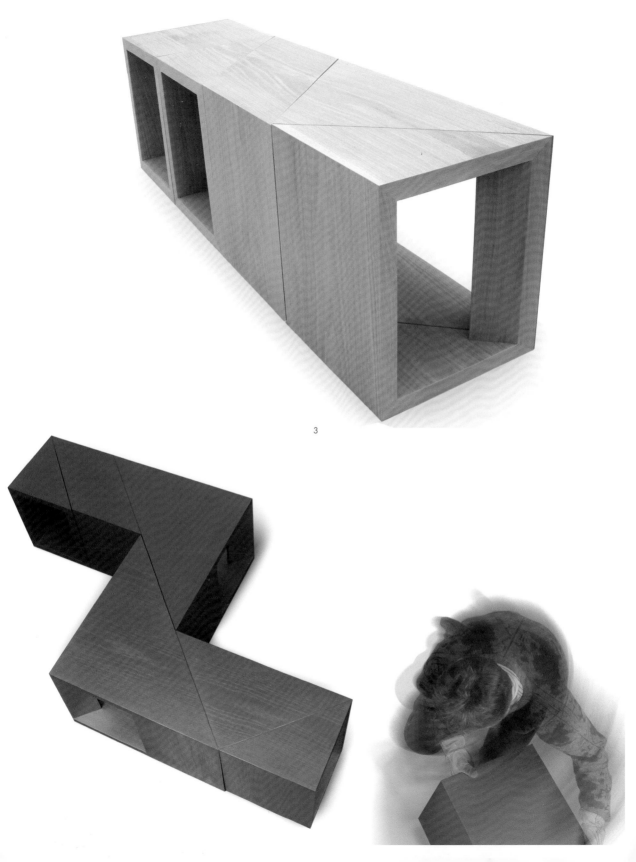

3

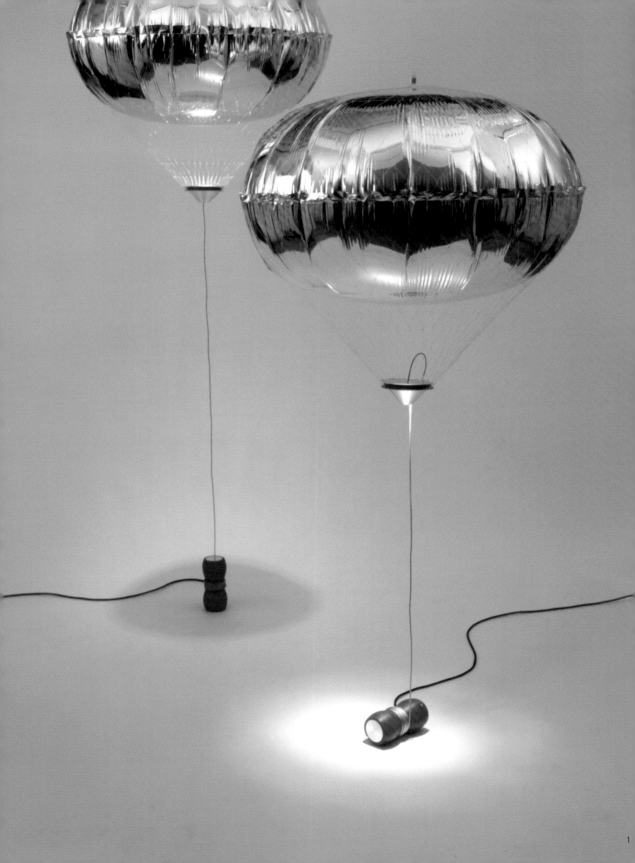

AFRODITI KRASSA INDUSTRIAL DESIGN CONSULTANTS | LONDON, UNITED KINGDOM
Afroditi Krassa

Afroditi Krassa is an award-winning designer consultancy including its own product line.
Their work is supported by an inimitable innovation structure, based on professional relationships between the creative team and clients.

www.afroditi.com

1 World View
2 Love Seat one
3 Eduardo's Light
4 Pretty big
5 In Plane english one
6 Bright Lights two

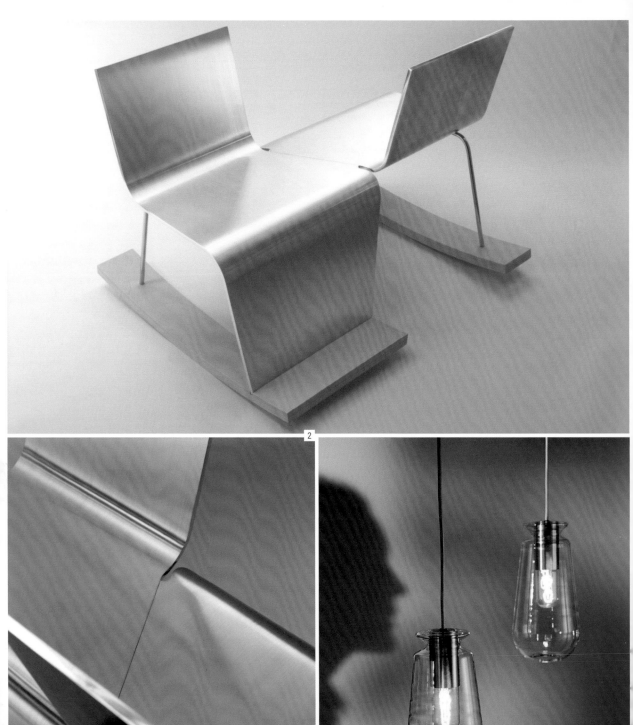

AHN AND AHN INDUSTRIAL DESIGN I COMO, ITALY
Christian von Ahn

International brands repeatedly rely on the services of Ahn and Ahn. Settled in the vicinity of several production firms, the agency develops products and accessories for the furniture and lighting industry.

www.ahnandahn.com

1 Spor
2 Cell, *pouf*
3 Cup
4 Gemini
5 Private Shpere, *Fishbowl*
6 Dyne

2

3

4

5

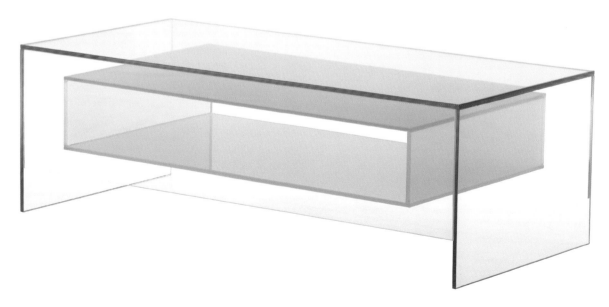

6

ALL-INTERIEUR | GEEL, BELGIUM
Stijn Schauwers

Stijn Schauwers began as an interior decorator for homes, shops and offices. With KAMELEON, he now presents his simple and versatile furniture projects.

www.all-interieur.be

Kameleon, *system furniture*

JULIAN APPELIUS BÜRO FÜR PRODUKTDESIGN | BERLIN, GERMANY
Julian Appelius

The office for product design is active in the areas of conception, object and graphic design as well as exhibition and trade-show design.

www.julianappelius.de

1 Kippel
2 Pixelwall
3 Halbe Portion 1

CLAUDIA SANTIAGO AREAL | DACHAU, GERMANY

Claudia Santiago Areal specializes in interiors, furniture and accessories that fluctuate between enjoyment, function and simplicity.

www.claudiasantiagoareal.de

1 Eclipse
2 Hugo
3 Edda

2

3

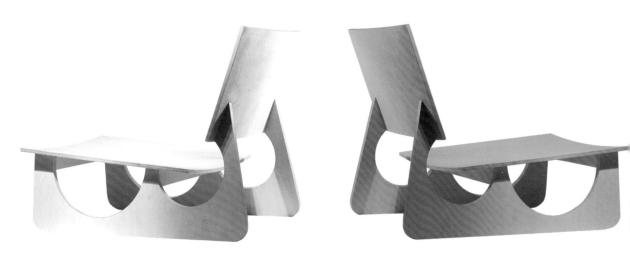

AUTOBAN | GALATA, TURKEY
Seyhan Özdemir, Sefer Çağlar

Autoban is an Istanbul-based architecture, interior design and product design studio, founded by Seyhan Özdemir (architect) and Sefer Çağlar (interior decorator) in the historic and bohemian district of Galata in 2003.

www.autoban212.com

1 Sledge
2 Sleepy
3 Deer
4 Starfish
5 Kahvechair
6 Spider
7 Lamba

3

4

5

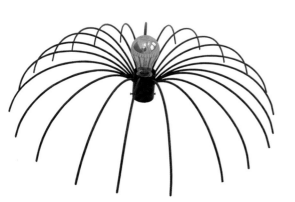

6

7

BARBER OSGERBY | **LONDON, UNITED KINGDOM**
Edward Barber, Jay Osgerby

Edward Barber and Jay Osgerby enjoy a growing reputation. They will discuss their recent work in products, furniture and interiors for Authentics, Cappellini, Magis and Stella McCartney, as well as future projects.

www.barberosgerby.com

1 Lunar
2 Shell Table & Stool
3 Paris
4 Portsmouth Bench
5 Flight Stool
6 Ipsei Bottle

2

3

4

5

6

BARNEY BARFORD | **LONDON, UNITED KINGDOM**

Barnaby Barford crosses and blurs the boundaries between art and design. He makes one-off ceramic pieces from mass manufactured or antique ceramic. His work is concerned with relationships and characteristics of everyday encounters.

www.barneybarford.co.uk

1 Don't worry darling, *you look fabulous*
2 The headless horseman
3 Mutton
4 Give me the carrots or the bunny gets it
5 I wish I was Hugh Hefner

2

3

4

5

ALBERTO BASAGLIA & NATALIA ROTA NODARI ARCHITETTI ASSOCIATI | BOLOGNA, ITALY

The works of Alberto Basaglia and Natalia Rota Nodari are directed toward holistic design concepts, and include the focal points architecture, interior design, design strategies, and product and graphic design.

www.ydf.it

1 Sofia Stool
2 Sciangai System, *sideboard*
3 Sciangai System, *bookcase*
4 Midollina
5 Margherita
6 Di Di, *system of hangers*

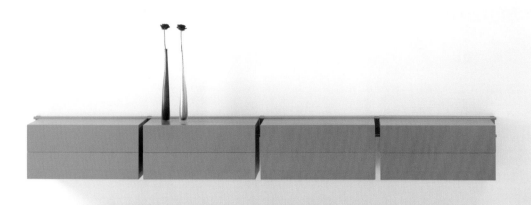

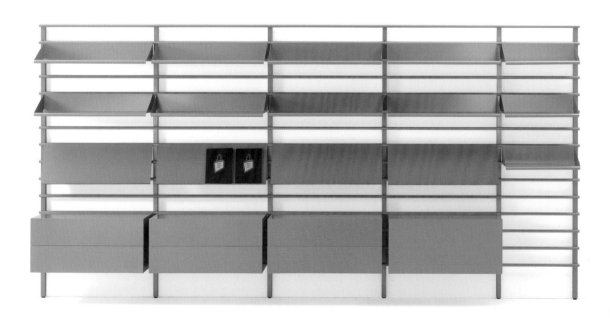

2

3

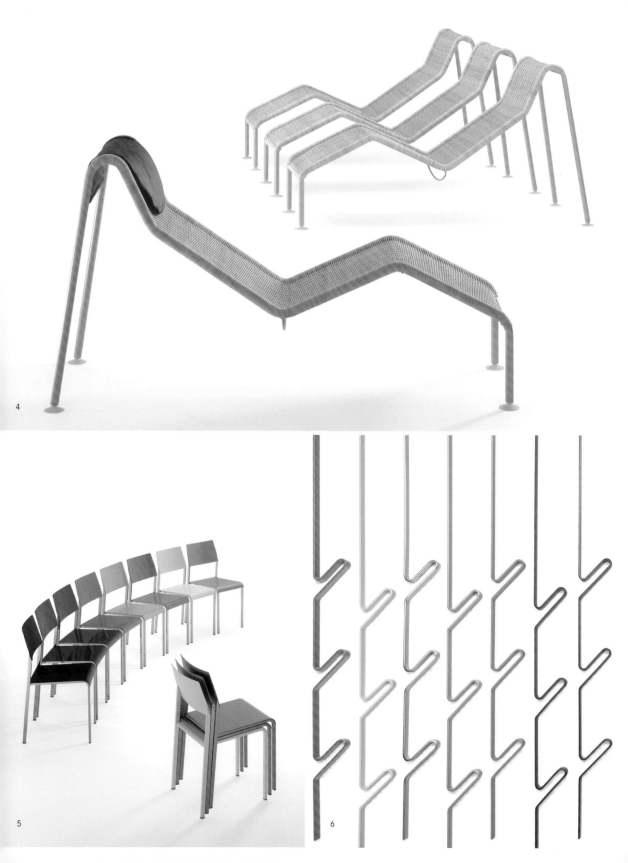

4

5

6

PAUL BECHSTEIN | BRACKENHEIM, GERMANY
Marcel Heinz

Marcel Heinz uses highly-demanding craftsmanship and his own language of shape to transform superior materials into fascinating figures.

www.paulbechstein.com

1 U-Hero motion, *adjustable high desk*
2 Chajin, *coffetable bench*
3 Sterces Neves, *cabinet with drawers*
4 Symphona Mano, *tone object*
5 BoB Juan, *screen/partition*
6 Ordaos, *cabinet on a tripod*
7 Search no more, *pencilholder*

2

3

4

5

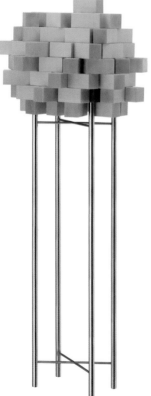

6

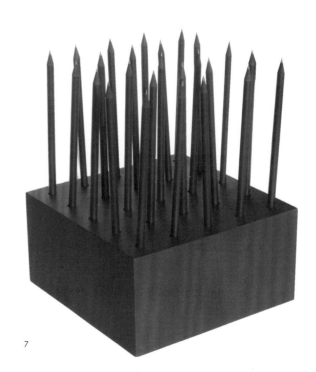

7

GABRIELA BELLON FURNITURE DESIGN | FRANKFURT, GERMANY

This native of Argentina worked as an architect and designer in Córdoba, Argentina, as well as Stuttgart, Munich and Frankfurt. She has her own furniture collection and also works as a designer on a commissioning basis.

www.gabrielabellon.com

1 Tres
2 Letras + Pura
3 Banco
4 Plata
5 Noah
6 Silencio
7 Luna, *bedside table*

bell
on

GABRIELA BELLON
FURNITURE DESIGN

3

4

5

6

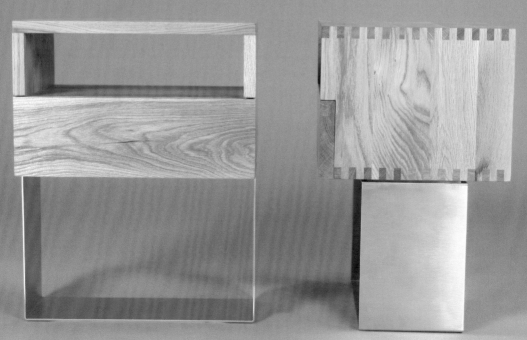

7

BERNSTRAND & CO | STOCKHOLM, SWEDEN
Thomas Bernstrand

Bernstrand & Co is now a design company working with product design, furniture design and interior design.

www.bernstrand.com

1 Thomas Bernstrand + do swing
2 Floor, *floor standing wine glass*
3 People
4 Self, *stackable shelf system*
5 Gobble, *coat hanger*
6 Bay Watch, *bikini life-jacket*
7 Hide

5

6

7

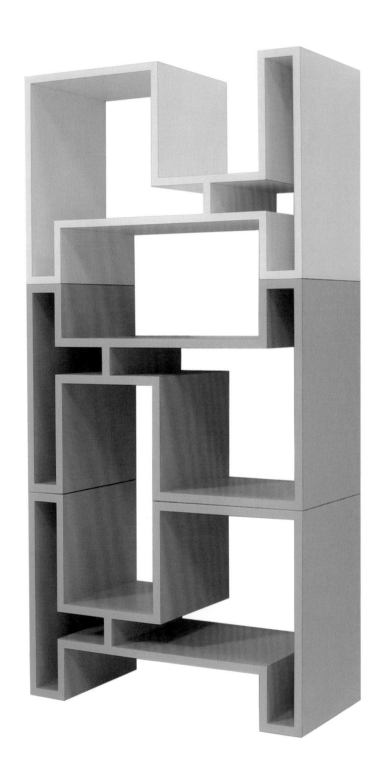

BERTELING DESIGN | **NOTRE DAME DE L'OSIER, FRANCE**
Yanine Berteling

Berteling Design creates and produces furniture and interior products characterized by simple and obvious shapes.

www.berteling-design.com

Upsido

MICHAEL BIHAIN INTERIOR & **FURNITURE DESIGN** | **BRUSSELS, BELGIUM**

Michaël Bihain has investigated the point of convergence of news, lifestyle, and conventional memories. The result is participation in customer appropriation.

www.michaelbihain.com

1 Oyon, *fruit holder*
2 Oyo
3 Cocofruit
4 Moon
5 Relax

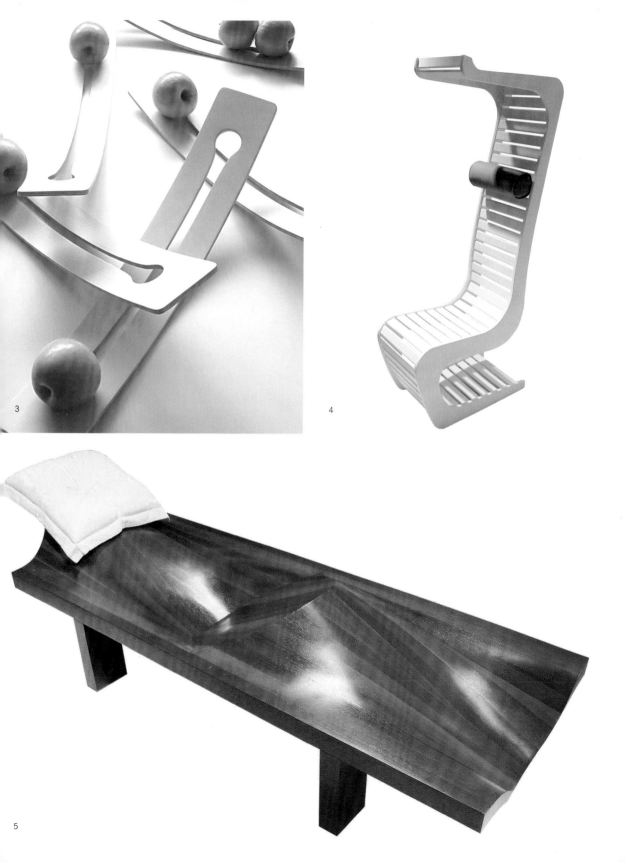

3

4

5

BKM DESIGN WORKING GROUP | VIENNA, AUSTRIA
Stefan Moritsch
Katharina Maria Bruckner
Herbert Klamminger

bkm Bruckner / Klamminger / Moritsch is a consortium that
employs the dissimilarities of its participants to create
award-winning products.

www.bkm-format.com

1 Falb
2 OneSquare
3 Buchhalter Drei

3

BRAM BOO | SINT-TRUIDEN, BELGIUM

Bram Boo, the Brussels-born designer, is currently working as an individual creative soul to create surprising things for micro and mass production.

www.bramboo.be

1 Orbit, *table with bar or desk*
2 Oasis, *modular couch with integrated desk and lamp*
3 Etcetera, *table with two included benches*
4 Loch Ness, *storage element with desk and
    stool included*

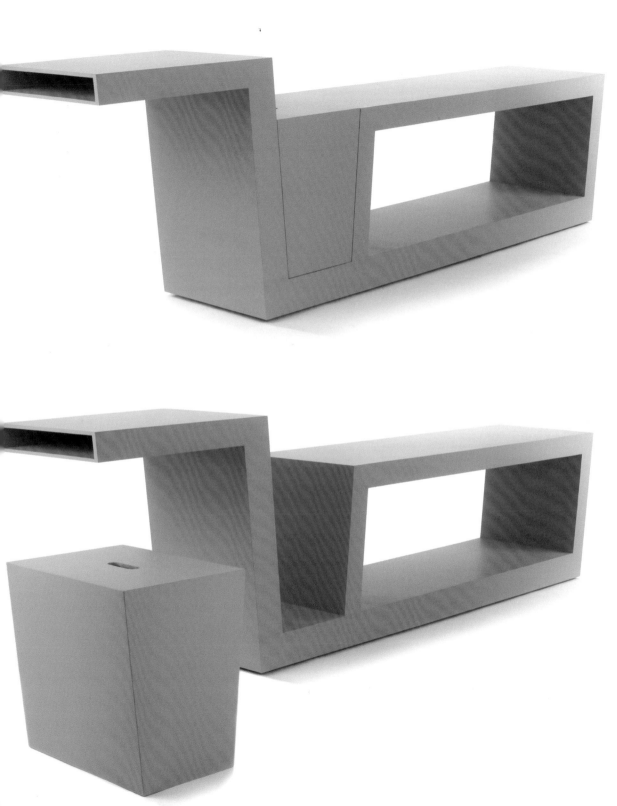

TODD BRACHER STUDIO | **PARIS, FRANCE**
Todd Bracher

His work experience spans the USA, Europe and now
the Far East. He has served as a consultant for various
studios in Copenhagen, Denmark, Milan, Italy, and London,
England. His tasks ranged from consumer products, store
planning to graphic design work, furniture, exhibition and
urban design.

http://go.to/toddbracher

1 Ideeover
2 Bloom
3 Openprev
4 Freud
5 Ideesoft

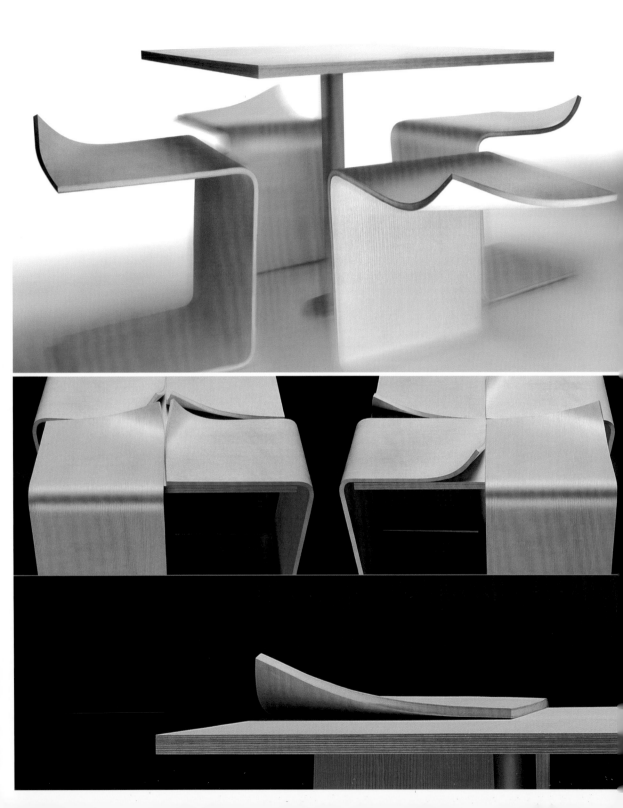

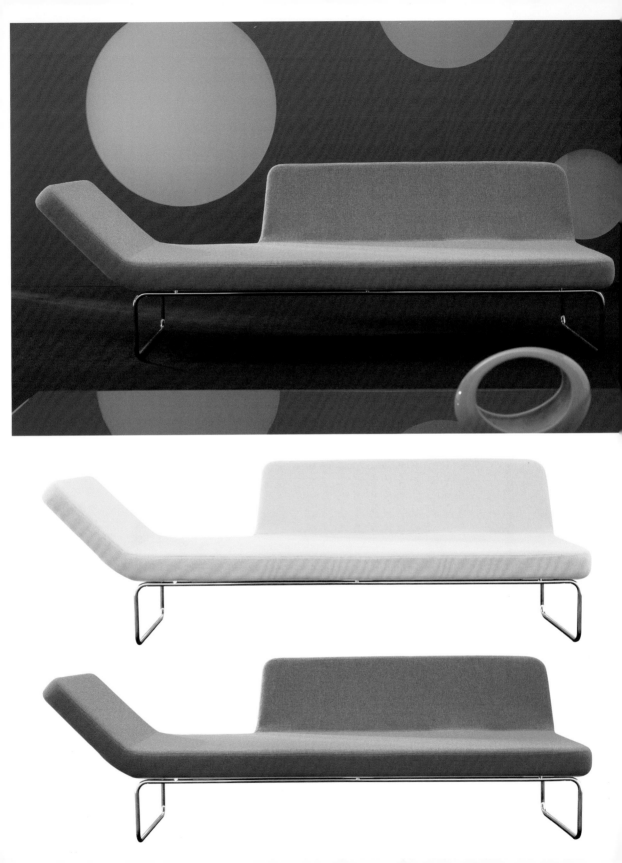

BURO BRUNO | ARNHEM, THE NETHERLANDS
Bruno van Hooijdonk

Buro bruno is a design studio for furniture and interior decoration products of original origins. Their products are based on research, experiment and a quest for form.

www.burobruno.nl

1 Rosy
2 Leonardo
3 Tulip
4 Dahlia
5 Molly
6 Lilly
7 Spin

2

3

4

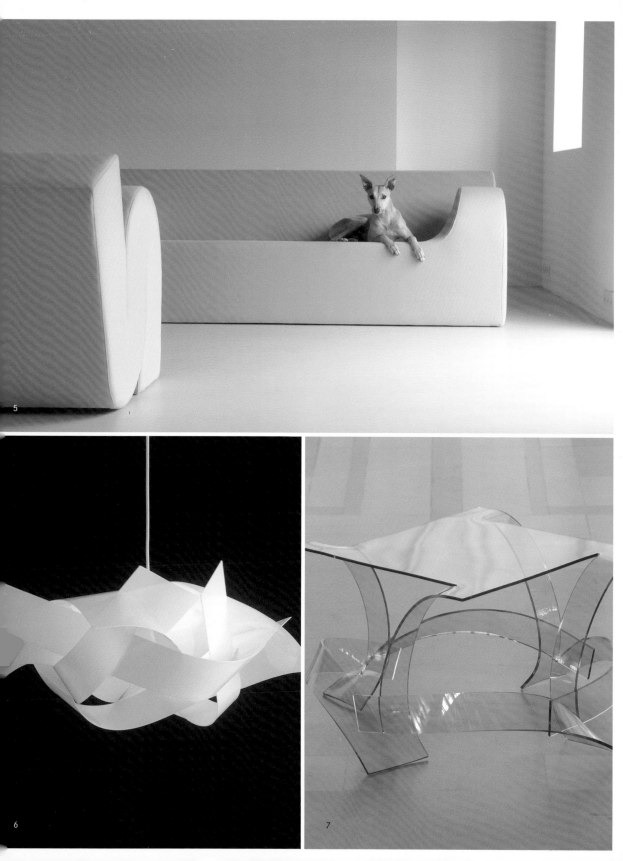

5

6

7

LOUISE CAMPBELL | COPENHAGEN, DENMARK

The studio specializes in furniture and product design. Its
focus is on finding new ways of designing familiar objects.

www.louisecampbell.com

1 Fatso
2 LP Balls
3 Honesty
4 Lamp for Danish Ministry of Culture
5 Between two chairs

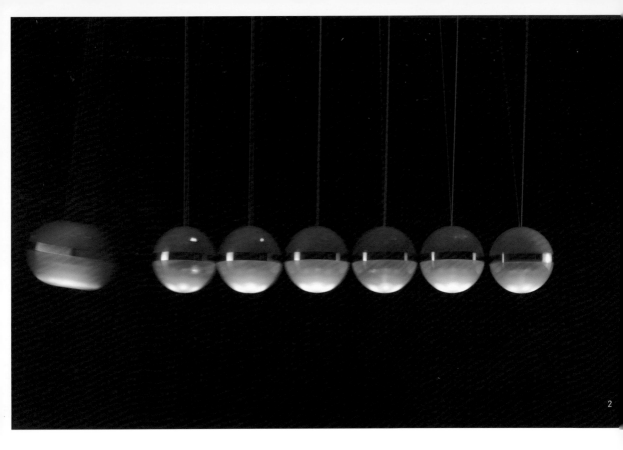

3

4

5

CHD INDUSTRIAL & PRODUCT DESIGN I **ATHENS, GREECE**
Constantinos Hoursoglou

chd is a multidisciplinary design consultancy aiming to
address the contemporary characteristics of human life.

www.chd.gr

1 Spice, *salt & pepper set*
2 Medal Case
3 Oda
4 Rouge, *3D puzzle*

2

3

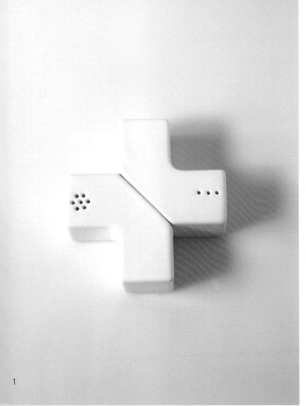

1

4

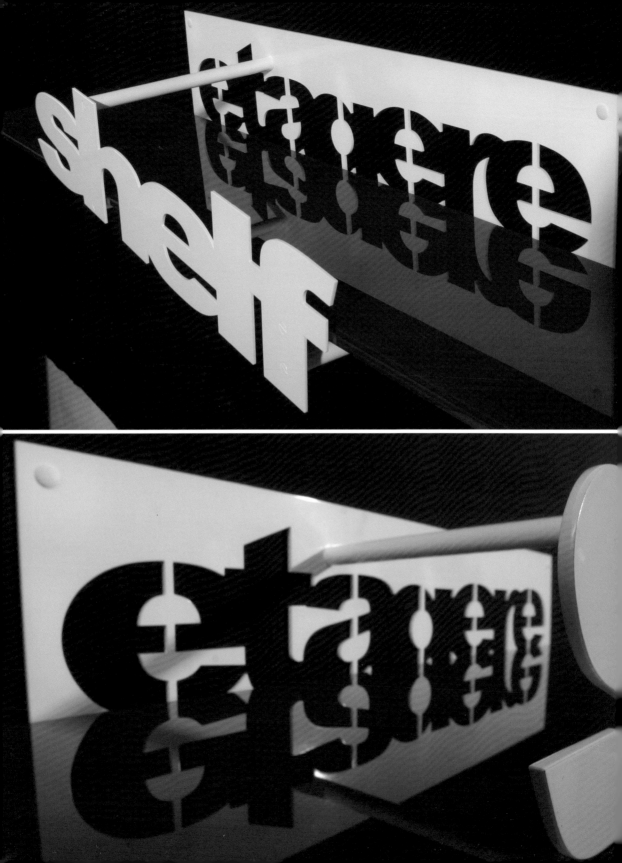

CIPRE DESIGN | NICE, FRANCE
Daniel Thiery

Stemming from the transfer of artistic work of Cipre
Sculpteur, the furniture design reflects the concept of the
artist of the new technologies to realize limited editions.

www.cipre.fr

1 Saisie
2 Console
3 Capture

CODE.2.DESIGN | STUTTGART, GERMANY
Michael Schmidt

His concepts are based on the idea that design is a strategically important element in the successful market positioning of a company. He believes in multidisciplinary project teams to turn innovative ideas into manufacturable and marketable solutions.

www.code2design.de

1 Solid Surface
2 Live Evolution
3 Tension
4 Hotspot

2

3

CONFUSED COLLECTION KONZEPTION UND GESTALTUNG | BERLIN, GERMANY
Sascha Akkermann
Elke Florian
Claudia Schramma
Martina Zeyen

Confused Collection is an open design network that provides an opportunity to get to know other ways of work and to form a creative symbiosis with others.

www.confused-collection.de

1 lks
2 Soft Sitty
3 Odu

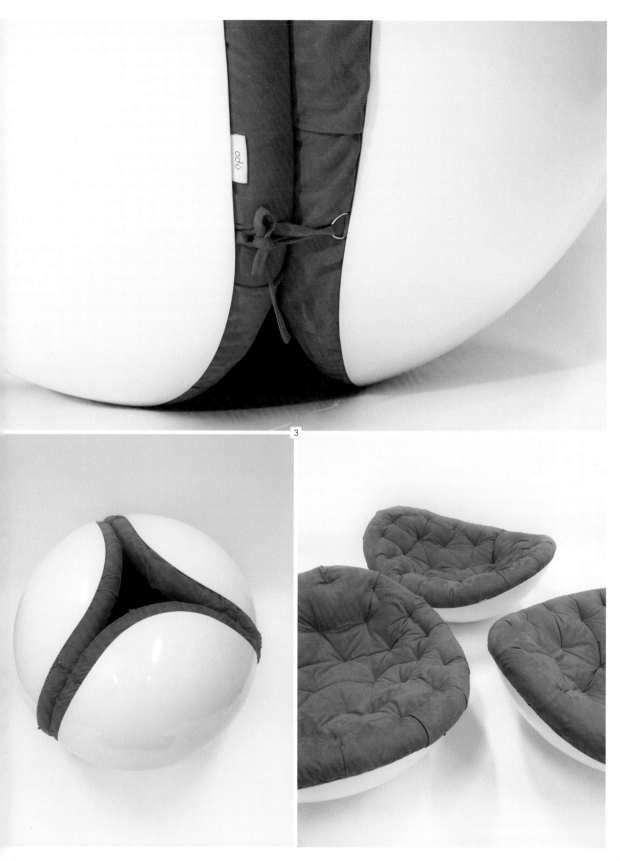

3

CROSS|CREATIVE DESIGNSTUDIOS | PFORZHEIM, GERMANY
Tom Nassal, Manuel Aydt

Crosscreative is a design team for products, concepts, packaging
and graphics. Fresh, stylish and fully equipped with high-
technology, a high level of competence and experience.

www.crosscreative.de

New Bobby Car

DANIELS & KOITZSCH DESIGNER I DARMSTADT, GERMANY
Micha Daniels, Stefan Koitzsch

Adding sensuousness to clarity, refinement to purity.

www.daniels-koitzsch.de

1 Espresso Machine
2 Pan Handle
3 Silverware
4 Espresso Machine
5 Telephone

2

3

4

5

MARIA DE ROS | BARCELONA, SPAIN

The studio's projects are characterized by their functionality and by an awareness of the social and physical environment, with an eye to ecology.

mariaderos@hotmail.com

Installation

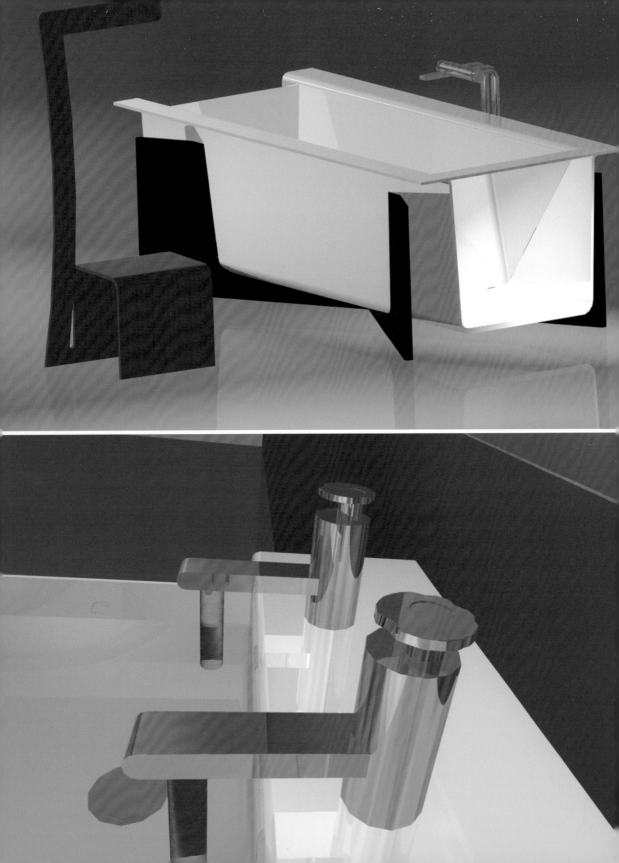

CÉDRIC DEBATTY | FLÉMALLE, BELGIUM

This firm's multifaceted, creative activities are to be understood as a permanent evolution, an active striving toward the unification of various design approaches and a holistic synergy.

cedricdebatty@skynet.be

1 Bathtub
2 Bath Fittings
3 Stool and Chair
4 Table view of the assembling
5 Valet
6 The Mirror

3

4

DEFACTO.DESIGN | MUNICH, GERMANY
Nikolaus Hartl, Hannes Weber

defacto.design was founded directly after our studies in 1996 in Munich. Since that time, we have worked for several companies all over the world.

www.defactodesign.de

1 Sledcarving
2 Lümmel
3 Lola
4 Kerzen: Notlicht, Zeitzünder, Advent
5 Kreis & Kreuz
6 Crosstable

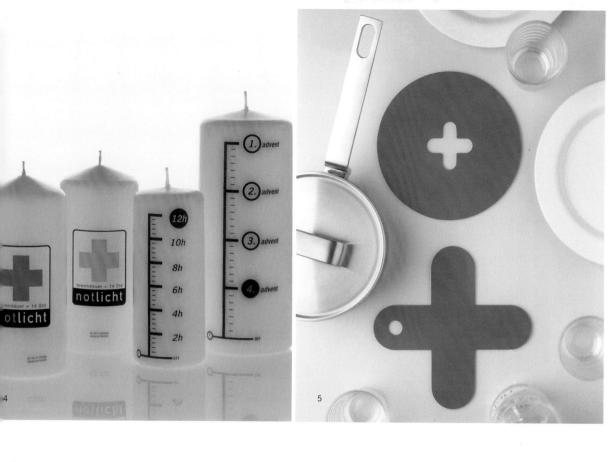

DEJANEW | PRAGUE, CZECH REPUBLIC
Gabriela Náhlíková, Leona Matějková

Gabriela Náhlíková and Leona Matějková seek unconventional, formal aesthetic and market-friendly design solutions with a high degree of acceptance.

www.dejanew.cz

Leto 2003, *lamp*

DELINEODESIGN | **MONTEBELLUNA, ITALY**
Giampaolo Allocco

Delineodesign was born from the desire to create a team of young creative individuals with precise characteristics: a good cultural base, very dynamic, in search of precision and maximum open-mindedness towards what is new.

www.delineodesign.it

1 Arancio
2 Simpaty
3 360°
4 Twenty
5 TricTrap

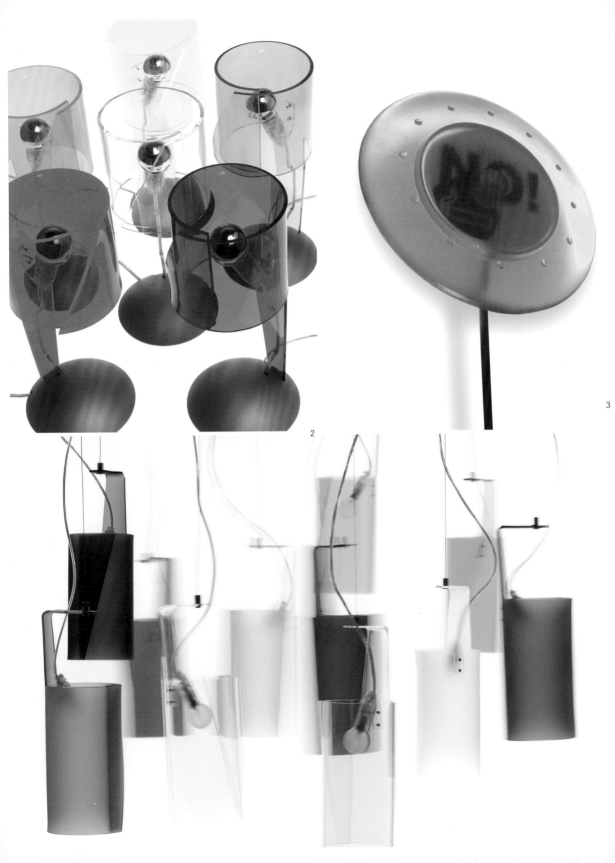

2

3

4

5

DESIGN AID | **PRAGUE, CZECH REPUBLIC**
Daria Podboj

Design Aid is a creative studio that brings together skills in interior decoration, graphic communication, urban design, signage, scenography and architecture for events.

dariapodboj@centrum.cz

1 Ruce
2 Stul

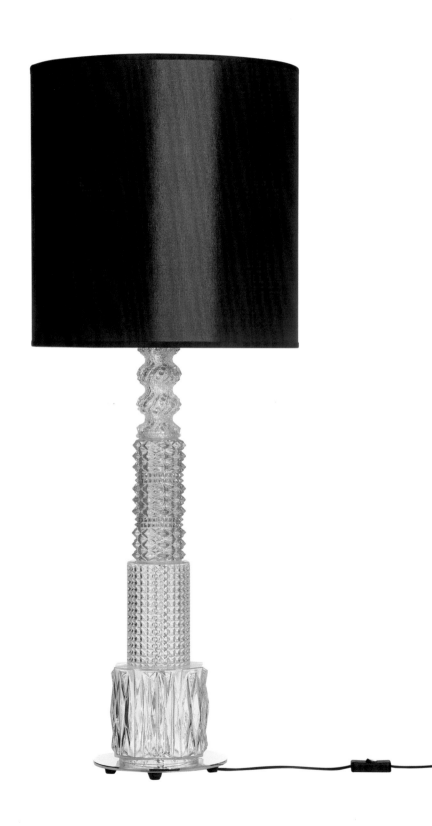

DESIGN BY US | **COPENHAGEN, DENMARK**
Rasmus Larsson, Ralph van der Made, Helene Strand, Lisette Rützoo

Design-by-us is a team of international, dynamic
designers that inspires with innovative and vibrant design.

www.design-by-us.com

1 Vintage Lamp
2 Infinity
3 Insect
4 Sild pendant
5 Pussy Chair
6 Skarpa

3

4

6

LILIAN DE SOUZA | KARLSRUHE, GERMANY

Life is guided by emotions, which in turn give birth to needs from which objects are defined. Lilian de Souza works in different fields of design, such as product, interior and furniture design.

www.liliandesouza.net

Simple Sound

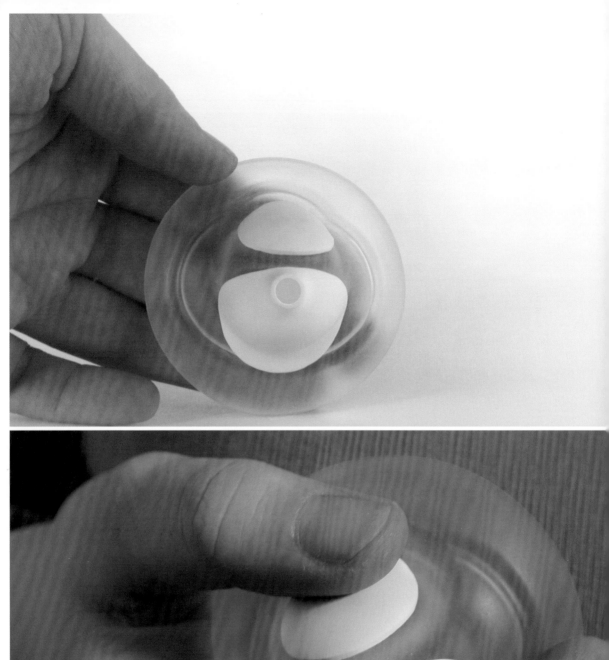
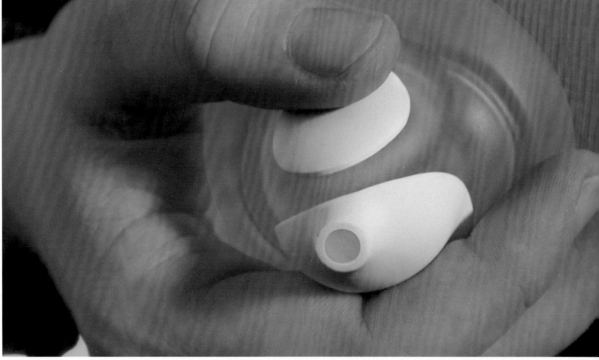

STEPHANIE DIETMANN | **FRANKFURT, GERMANY**

Lucky Strike Junior Designer Award 2004 – honorable mention, Mia Seeger Prize 2004 – honorable mention + Mia Seeger Most Promising Award, if Design Award 2005 concepts winner, International Dyson Blue Print Award 2005 "Global Dyson Blueprint Trophy"

stephanie.dietmann@gmx.net

Breast Pump for Mother's Milk

STEFAN DIEZ | MUNICH, GERMANY

Stefan Diez is an often awarded industrial designer.
He was assistant designer for Richard Sapper in the US
and Konstantin Grcic in Munich; in 2003 he opened his
own studio.

www.stefan-diez.com

1 Pots
2 Buoy, *dispenser*
3 Big Bin
4 Instant Lounge

3

4

5

DISORDER COLLECTIV | KORTRIJK, BELGIUM
Robin Delaere

Robin Delaere runs the Disorder Collectiv studio, together with Jan Kindt. The Collectiv primarily focuses on commercializing its own designs. Since its launch, the Collectiv has grown into a design and manufacturing company that produces furniture as well as smaller objects and even posters.

www.disorder.be

1 Twice
2 Sunlounger
3 Brainibox
4 Chill
5 Pouf

2

3

4

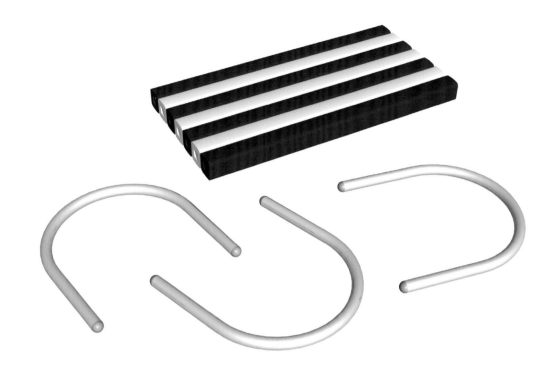

5

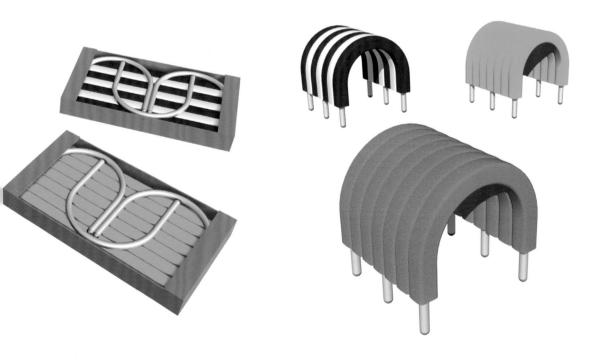

ELEMENT DESIGN | VIENNA, AUSTRIA
Stephan Breier, Johannes Scherr

Nowadays, element design works principally in the fields of product, packaging and transportation design. Their packaging design activities have included various projects for beverage companies.

www.element.co.at

coffice

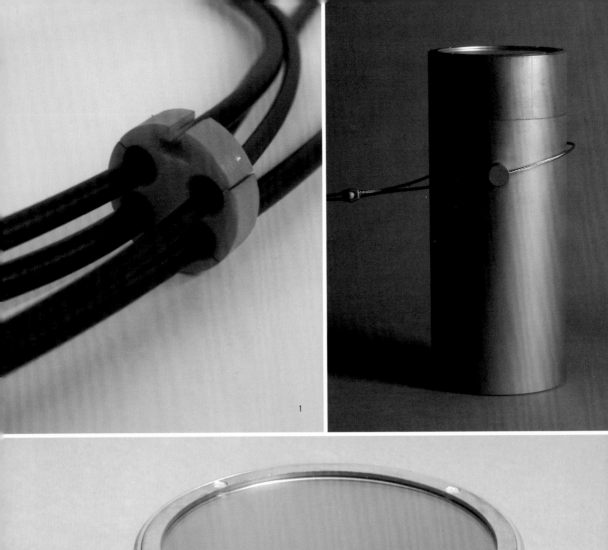

1

FASHIONSTEEL MÖBELDESIGN | BASEL, SWITZERLAND
Alban Schär, Lukas Pfister

Alban Schär and Lukas Pfister began building tables, beds and chairs out of necessity. They have remained true to their line and yet perpetually modern ever since. Simple, elegant and rich in contrast.

www.fashionsteel.ch

1 Cablerouter, *cable manager for the desktop*
2 Urn
3 Urn detail, *room for a dowry*

FEINEDINGE* HANDMADE PRODUKTGESTALTUNG | VIENNA, AUSTRIA
Sandra Haischberger

feinedinge* handmade produktgestaltung is specialized in the design and generation of prototypes made of porcelain, as well as the manufacture of small series.

www.feinedinge.at

1 Tapas
2 Flow

FIFTY-EIGHT B | DUBLIN, IRELAND
Lorraine Blennan

The award winning design studio Fifty-Eight b designs,
manufacturers and supplies both collection and specially
made contemporary interior products for industry,
architects, developers, manufacturers, specifiers, retailers
and private clients.

www.fiftyeightb.ie

1 Bedroom Range
2 Low Coffee Table
3 Drawer Cabinet
4 Polly Pendant
5 Fruit Bowl
6 Dinning Table

5

6

FILE STUDIO | PRAGUE, CZECH REPUBLIC
Jan Čtvrtnik

File Studio creates and updates client identity to increase the impact of your industrial production and differentiate yourself from competitors.

www.file-studio.com

Koxy

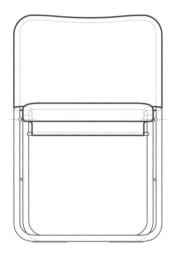

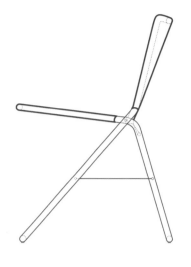

FOR USE | VIENNA, AUSTRIA
Sven Jonke, Christoph Katzler, Nikola Radeljkovic

Industrial design is realized under the name For Use;
interiors, exhibitions, scenographies and events under
Numen.

www.foruse.info

1 SMLX
2 HPLC
3 L_2
4 FU06
5 HPL

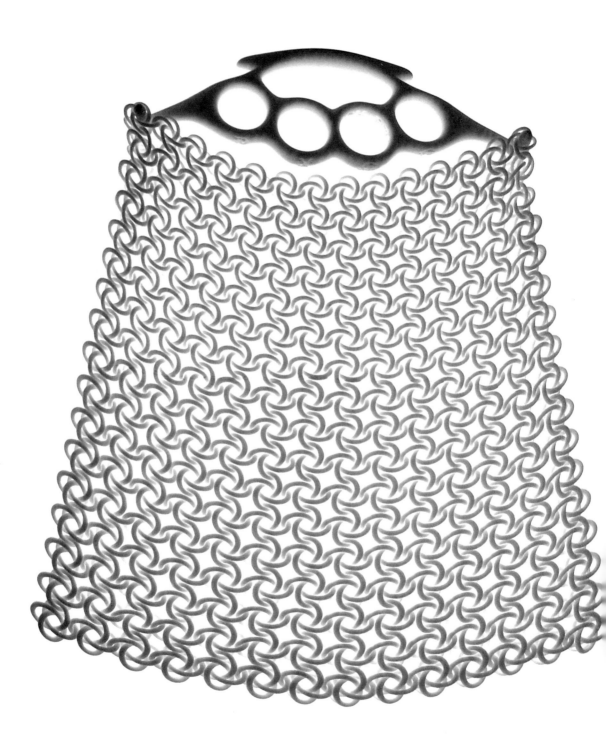

FREEDOM OF CREATION | AMSTERDAM, THE NETHERLANDS

FOC is where cutting edge technology meets design. FOC is a research and design company working on projects for companies, research organizations and universities who have similar goals to ours, but need design and manufacturing consultation in order to reach these goals.

www.freedomofcreation.com

Punchbag

FREMDKÖRPER | COLOGNE, GERMANY
Andrea Mehlhose, Martin Wellner

Fremdkörper works with a focus on comprehensive inter-disciplinary design solutions.

www.solutionsfornoproblem.com

Netto

FRONT | STOCKHOLM, SWEDEN
Sofia Lagerkvist, Charlotte von der Lancken,
Anna Lindgren, Katja Sävström

Front is a four women design group. Front questions
distinctions between art and design, between functional and nonfunctional objects, and even between
dead objects and living beings.

www.frontdesign.se

1 Surroundings Vase
2 Snake Hangers
3 Insect Table
4 Rat Wallpaper
5 Pressure

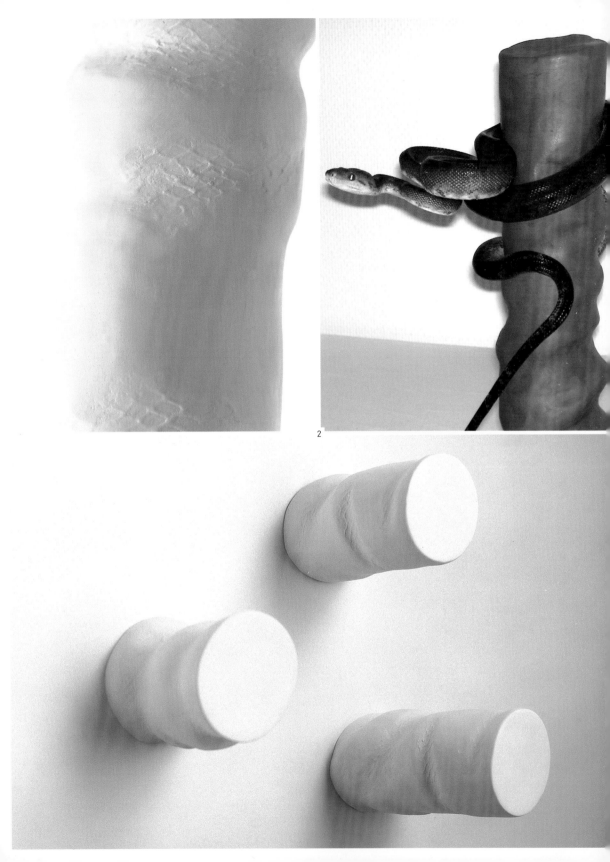

2

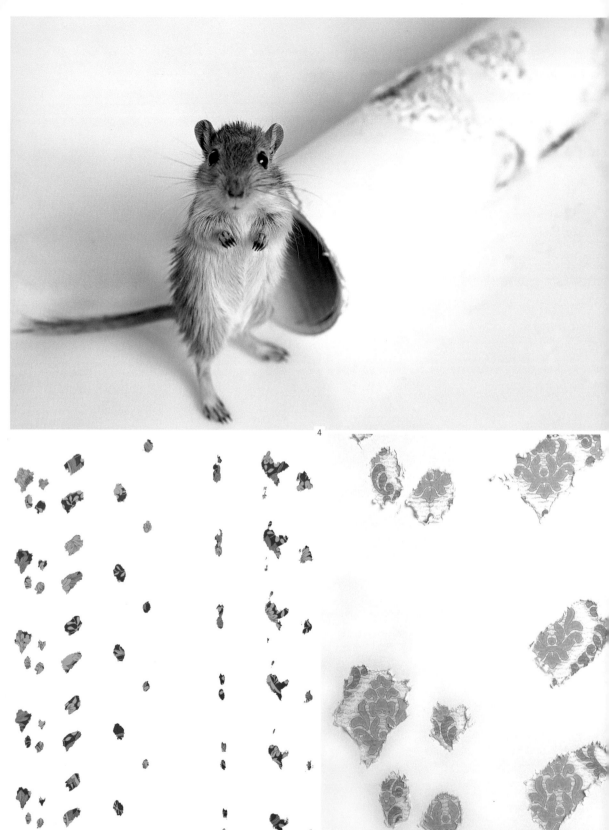

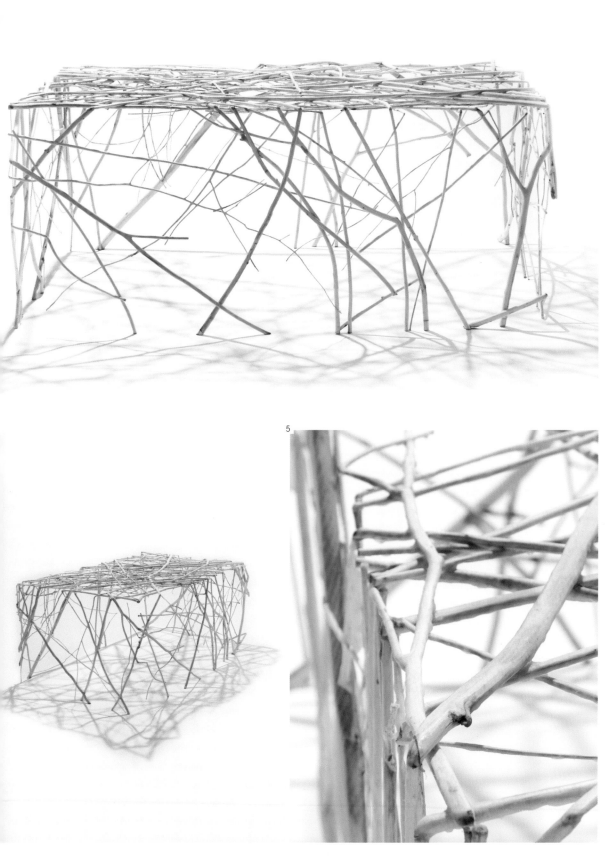

5

JÖRG GÄTJENS DESIGN DEVELOPMENT | **COLOGNE, GERMANY**

Gätjens deals with finding new connections in form and material and the development of innovative design and products.

www.joerg-gaetjens.com

1 cutlery
2 magnetic table, *individual table system*
3 "Kleiner Lehrer", *writing stand*

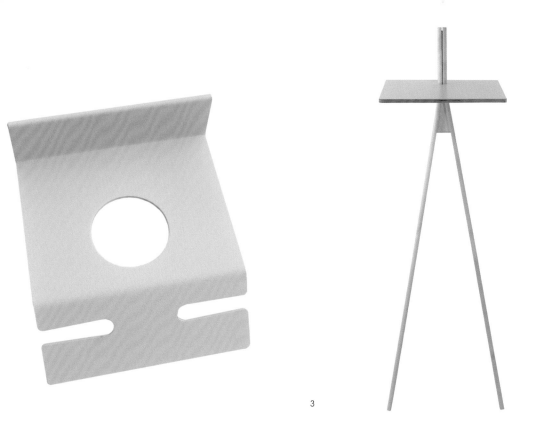

3

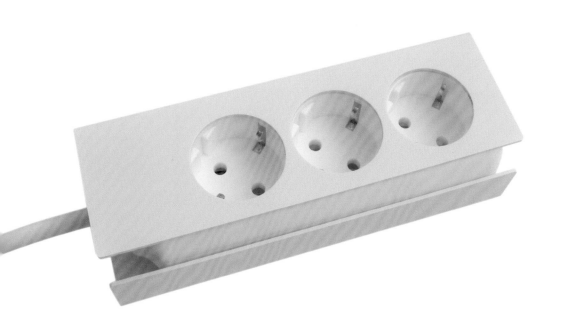

GODART DESIGNERS | PARIS, FRANCE

Laurent Godart, Vanessa Godart

Their work focuses on objects that are part of everyday life. They aim at making everyday movements more simple, more pleasant and more personal.

godart.designers@aol.com

Soliflore Atoflore

CAMILLA GROTH | **HELSINKI, FINLAND**

Camilla Groth is specialized in ceramics and glass design and works as a freelance designer from her studio in Helsinki.

camillagroth@hotmail.com

1 section vases
2 lens bowls
3 section bowls
4 red cup & table set

GRUPPE RE | **COLOGNE, GERMANY**
Nicole Hüttner, Silke Warchold

Nicole Hüttner and Silke Warchold industrially produce materials, rediscover old and the latest materials in their interior and product design.

www.gruppe-re.de

1 L 101, Lightning design, *for the hotel ku¹damm 101*
2 'corso', *illuminating wallpaper*
3 glasstable, *phosphorescent glass*

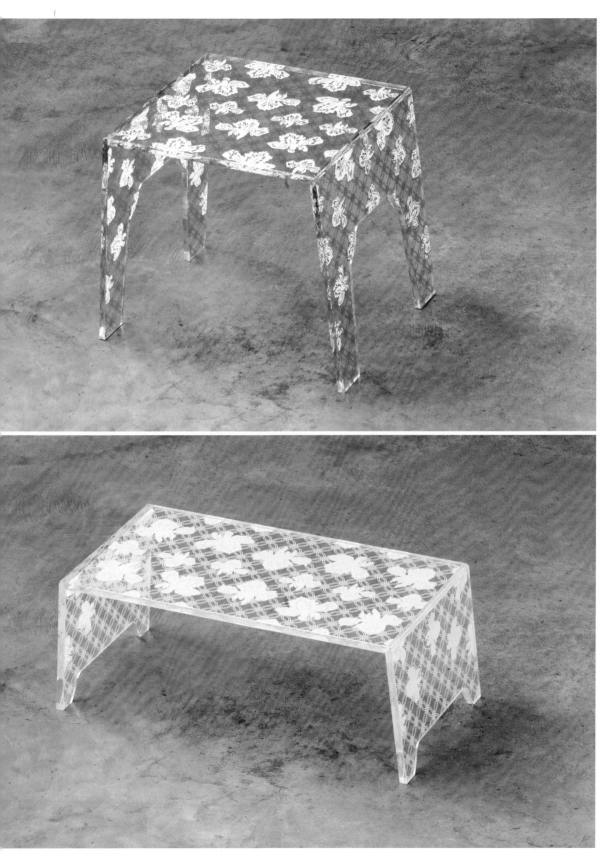

DOUG HARPER FURNITURE | LONDON, UNITED KINGDOM

Doug Harper seeks to offer durable, cohesive, useful, visually pleasing and versatile solutions.

www.hiddenart.com

1 Litables D-ended table
2 Series T

HIPPOS DESIGN ARCHITEKTURA | PRAGUE, CZECH REPUBLIC
Radim Bobák, Andrej Tobola

The hippos studio was founded in 2003 by Radim Babak and Ondrej Tobola in Prague. It concentrates primarily on product/interior design and architecture.

www.hipposdesign.com

1 Standing lamp
2 Electric iron concept
3 Peugeot concept
4 Soft 3

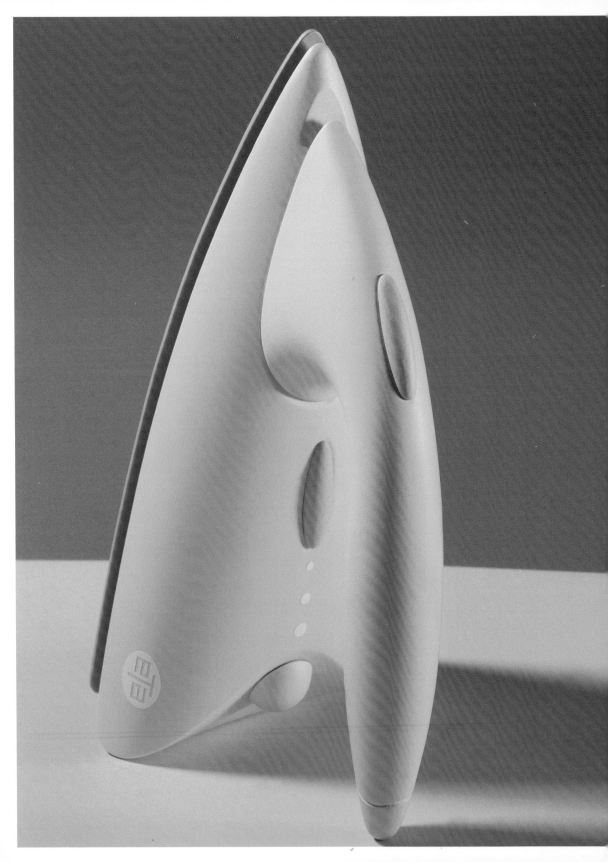

IL-STUDIO | AMSTERDAM, THE NETHERLANDS
Isabelle Leijn

iL-studio is an Amsterdam-based design company that
has specialized in interior decoration and furniture since
1996. The designs have a monumental and architectonic
look.

www.il-studio.nl

1 A vase (for victory or memorial?)
2 Goldfish Racetrack
3 Bank 002
4 Sling

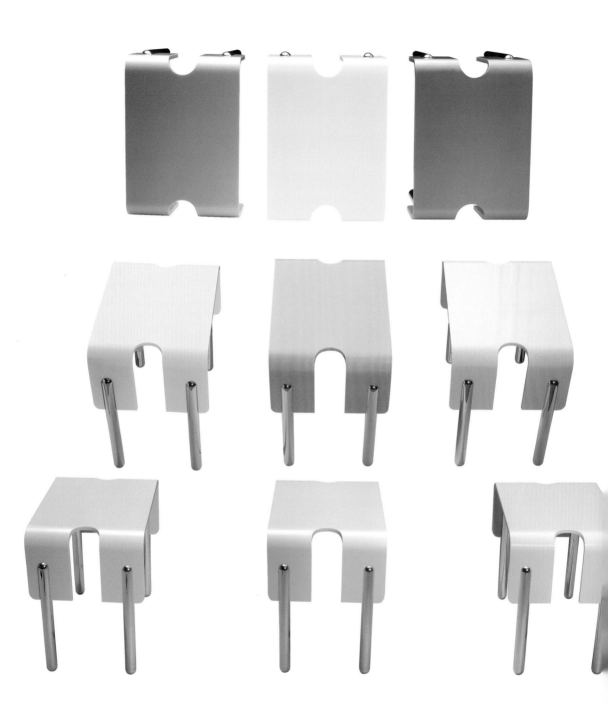

INSTANTCONCEPT BUERO FÜR GESTALTUNG, DESIGN, INNENARCHITEKTUR | WUPPERTAL, GERMANY
Jörg Berghäuser

Instantconcept is an interdisciplinary design office with a focus on furniture, object and product design as well as the development of new ideas for representative space concepts.

www.instantconcept.com

1 Ahab
2 1zu1
3 Reiko

IRION MÖBELSYSTEME | WINTERTHUR, SWITZERLAND
Stefan Irion

Since 1996, Stefan Irion has conducted his own model construction and product development studio. Since 2000, the young designer has presented his "Irion Furniture System" – products made from birch plywood without compromise in quality.

www.irion.li

Zwei Kammern breit

FLORENCE JAFFRAIN | **PARIS, FRANCE**

Twelve years designing at the service of leading labels (Hermès, Saint Louis, Paco Rabanne, Peugeot, Long-champ ...), have enabled Florence Jaffrain to perfect her eye and acquire the technical knowledge necessary for producing her own creations.

www.moaproduction.com

1 Full Moon
2 Face2Face
3 Love
4 Wave

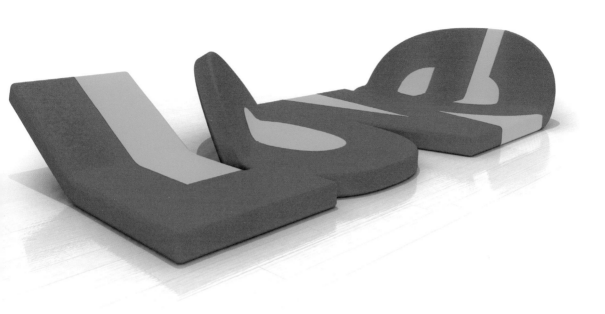

JEHS + LAUB | STUTTGART, GERMANY
Markus Jehs, Jürgen Laub

Ever since they both studied product design, Markus Jehs and Jürgen Laub have been creating domestic furniture, lamps, kitchens, shops and trade show stands.

www.jehs-laub.de

1 Blox
2 Big Blox
3 4000
4 Leo

KAFKA.DESIGN | BERLIN, GERMANY
Cordula Kafka

Tracing the material – kafka.design is the capacity to re-conceive the nature of substance and use it in an original context.

www.kafkadesign.de

1 Thincut
2 Solas
3 Blast

1

2

3

STUDIO MONNI KARRI | HELSINKI, FINLAND

The area of activity of Studio Monni Karri extends well beyond furniture and product design. It includes thorough consultation in design management and creative and design services.

www.lapalma.it

1 Thin
2 Laaka
3 Thin S 17

KIK! | EINDHOVEN, THE NETHERLANDS
Kiki van Eijk

Kik! has been active in the design field since 2001. She works on her own collection which is presented in international galleries and museums, as well as for projects for companies, institutions and individuals.

www.kikiworld.nl

Fashion ceramics

HEALTH

the first aid set. with a smile design. michael koenig

MICHAEL KOENIG | **HAMBURG, GERMANY**

The studio works on projects in the areas of furniture, accessories, lighting and interior design.

www.studiomichaelkoenig.com

1 Health, *textile set*
2 Ben Hur, *magazine rack*
3 Gleam
4 Haeng rum

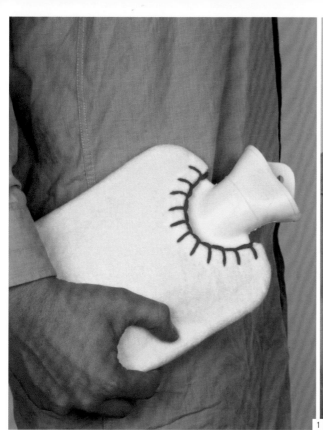

1

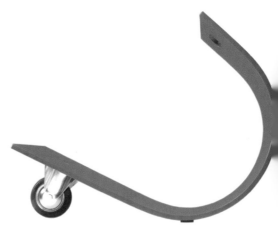

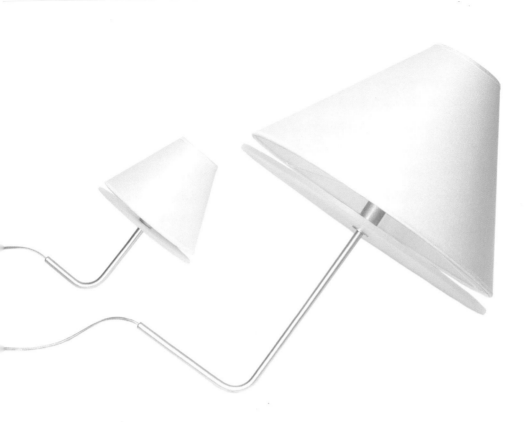

4

LIFESTYLE SPACE | **LONDON, UNITED KINGDOM**
Lee McCormack

The team Life Style Space is about pulling together many different ideas and turning them into something exciting.

www.theoculas.com

Okulas

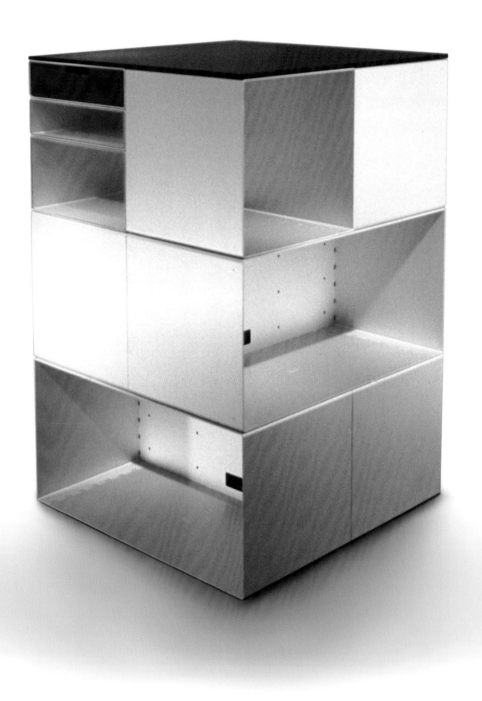

PATRICK LINDON | **OBERWIL BEI ZUG, SWITZERLAND**

Patrick Lindon proposes changing ideas, projects, style and collections by integrating an image and contemporary design resolutely aimed at the future.

www.patrick-lindon.com

Element Typ 71, *individual furniture system*

LORENZ * KAZ | MILAN, ITALY
Catharina Lorenz, Steffen Kaz

In addition to an array of now standard furniture and product lines, Lorenz * Kaz Creations also engage in specialty development projects and limited-edition specialty designs.

www.lorenz-kaz.com

Aspetto, *seating system*

FELIX SEVERIN MACK | ESSLINGEN, GERMANY

Felix Severin Mack is one of those designers for whom innovation and experimentation in furniture and lighting design is a significant component of the design process.

www.felix-severin-mack.com

1 Mesdames, *glasobjects handmade of colored leadglass*
2 Taurus, *cocktail cabinet*

MAYBE DESIGN | ISTANBUL, TURKEY
Susanne Akcay, Bora Akcay, Erdem Akan

maybe design was founded in 2003 in Istanbul and was focused on object design and furniture. maybe are not fixed on any one material; they are open to any material and material mix – and even to complete objects as raw material.

www.maybedesign.at

1 melange
2 shop-window dummyhands, *coathanger*
3 channel 5, *nightlamp*
4 winglet
5 glasses
6 east meets west, *teaglasses*

3

JULIA MAENDLER DESIGNER | PARIS, FRANCE

Julia Maendler's work is of the finest quality, reflecting her extensive experience in designing and production in recent years.

pixxpaxx@hotmail.com

Vase Cœur

MANZLAB | COPENHAGEN, DENMARK
Cecilie Manz

The Manzlab agency develops product strategies in the areas of design, development and realization of furniture and product design.

www.manzlab.dk

1 Ladder Hochacht
2 Fixed Seats
3 Micado Table

2

DESIGN BY F MAURER | VIENNA, AUSTRIA
Franz Maurer

design by f maurer focuses on product design, presentations and interior concepts, all of them with surprising elements.

www.fmaurer.com

1 Rita
2 Dance of the Glasses
3 Concave
4 Crack, *seats and tables*
5 Snow

3

5

MOMENTUM | **ZURICH, SWITZERLAND**
Sven Adolph

Sven Adolph designs products with a clear point of view.
Distinction, precision and coherence are key to his work.

www.momentumdesign.ch

1 Media Player CD/DVD
2 Loudspeakers
3 Ceramic Space Heater

MONICA GRAFFEO DESIGNER | ZOPPOLA DI PORDENONE, ITALY

Her work especially for furniture companies and my best interests involves materials and technologies applied to furniture.

www.monicagraffeo.it

1 Flow
2 Boum
3 Mints
4 cu

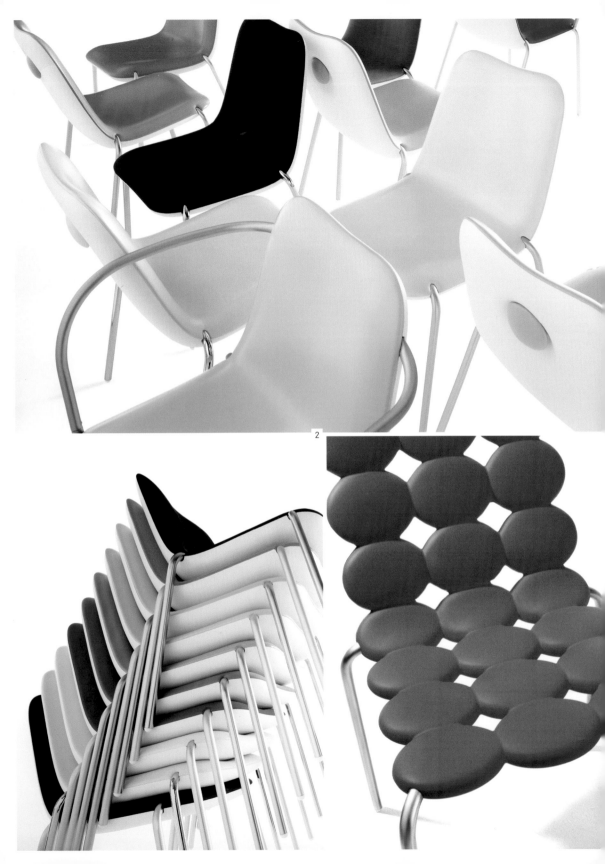

2

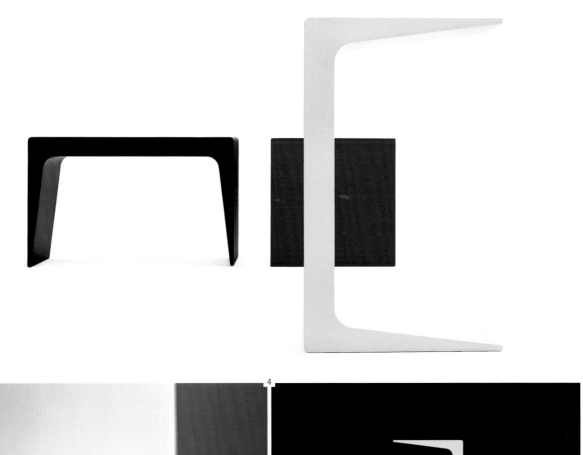

ROBERTO MONTE | PAGANI, ITALY

Each project is unique. There is no recipe, no style and no automatism in Monte's designing. His solution is then rigorously followed through with the appropriate methods and means.

www.m2design.it

Rubber lamp

WALTER MUSACCHI | BERLIN, GERMANY

The designer, who now lives in Berlin, has worked for several architectural agencies in Paris, Berlin, New York, Rotterdam, and Los Angeles, including for Jean Nouvel and Rem Koolhaas.

www.waltermusacchi.com

Wasserstand, *vase*

TORSTEN NEELAND | LONDON, UNITED KINGDOM

Torsten Neeland's projects range from cutlery design, to lighting, to interiors. His studio has been based in London since 1997.

www.torsten-neeland.co.uk

1 Tea egg
2 Stool – Side tables
3 Cutlery set
4 Bath tray

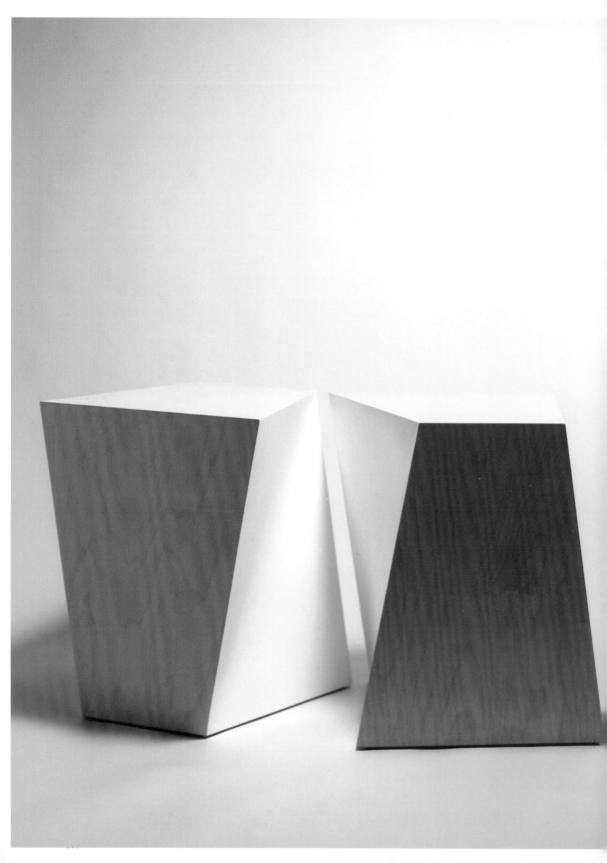

NEUSTAHL | LUCERNE, SWITZERLAND
Hanspeter Meyer

Linear, simple and pragmatic – the design of NEUSTAHL is characterized by clear forms and an uncompromising reduction to the essentials.

www.neustahl.ch

Bett 01

NICHETTO+GAI | VENICE, ITALY
Luca Nichetto, Gianpietro Gai

Spunklab claim create objects which "speak" to people: Speaking in a familiar language, they express brand new concepts without any further explanation. Their projects aim to make the user feel something new.

www.spunklab.it

1 Spoon
2 Specchio_ice-star
3 Office

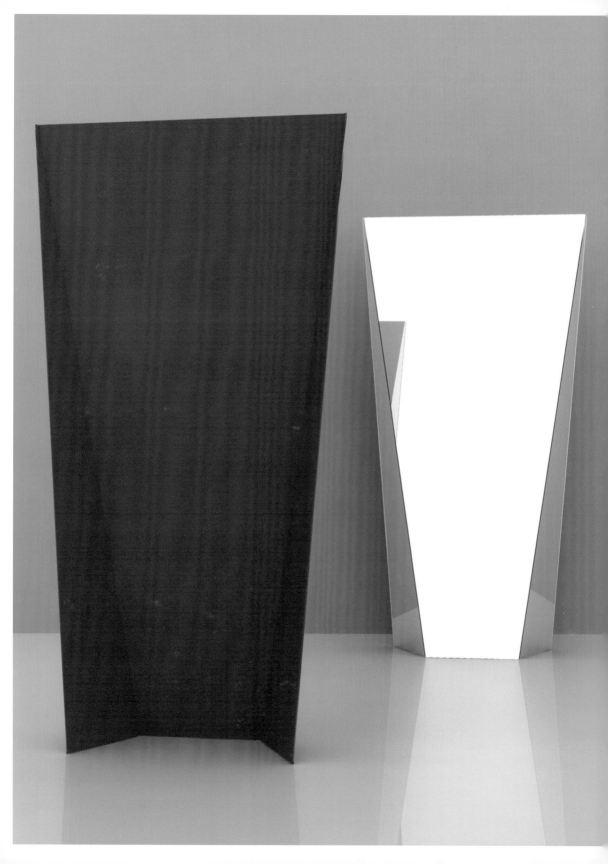

NIX | LONDON, UNITED KINGDOM
Annette Nix

Internationally renowned carpet queen Annette Nix
designs innovative and thought-provoking carpets to commission in any size, shape or color and can incorporate
such diverse materials as sheet metal, stones, water and
even live fish!

www.annettenix.com

1 Swirls
2 Bath Slate
3 White & Case

OLZE & WILKENS | BERLIN, GERMANY
Karen Olze, Gisa Wilkens

Olze & Wilkens focus on developing furniture and accessories that respond to peoples' behavior and everyday needs; they question habits, merge familiar objects and thereby gain new emotional and functional qualities.

www.olzewilkens.de

1 Showhide, *flexible lamella sheet*
2 flenndoch, *Pillow with an integrated tissue-package*

DIETER PAUL DESIGN | GRAZ, AUSTRIA

Areas of focus are high-quality folding and ergonomic seating furniture. Each design is a new beginning.

www.dipaul.com

1 Tombo
2 Sono
3 Balu

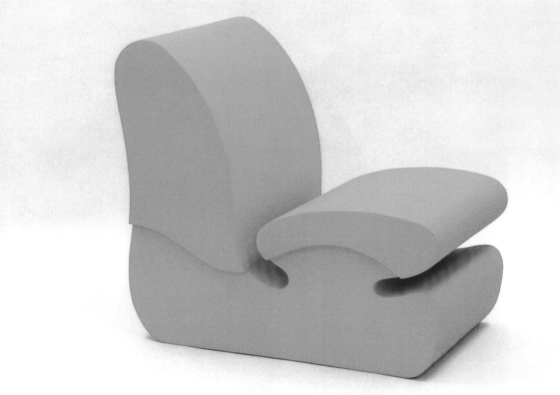

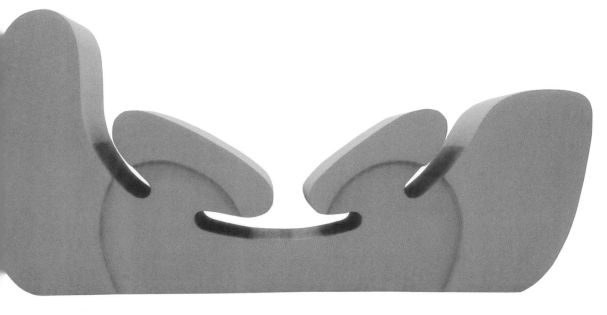

PEARSONLLOYD DESIGN | LONDON, UNITED KINGDOM
Luke Pearson, Tom Lloyd

Pearson Lloyd is multi-disciplinary design studio based in Central London. The studio's work focuses on design for manufacture, strategic brand development and research in the fields of Furniture, Transport Design and the Public Realm.

www.pearsonlloyd.co.uk

1 Turtle Dining
2 Cantilever chair
3 Aleos Lamp
4 Westminster Street Lightning

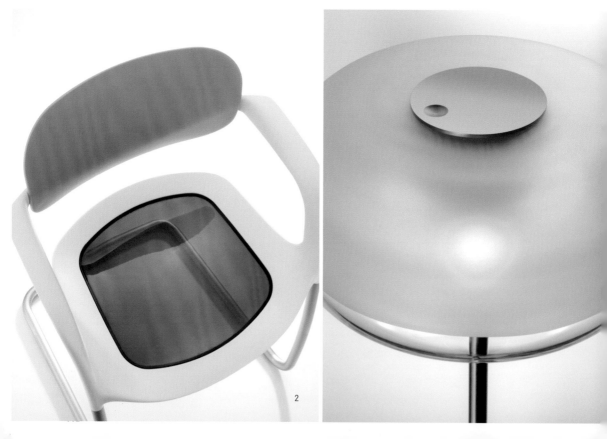

FLORIAN PETRI INDUSTRIAL DESIGN | BERLIN, GERMANY

Florian Petri was involved in the development of the "Mirra-Chair" for Herman Miller as well as in several design studies (Studio 7.5) and the "Plan-A" Sinterchair (Vogt+Weizenegger). The shelf system "platten_bau" was presented at imm cologne in 2004. It received the red dot design award "best of the best" in 2005.

www.fpid.de

Platten_Bau

THE PFEIFER CONSULTANCY | LONDON, UNITED KINGDOM
Leonhard Pfeifer

The Pfeifer Consultancy offers a consulting design service to industry, in addition to the growing range of standard products, furniture and domestic accessories, marketed under the "Pfeifer" brand.

www.leonhardpfeifer.com

1 Sushi Board
2 Roomset

POLKA PRODUCT PLEASURE | **VIENNA, AUSTRIA**
Marie Rahm, Monica Singer

Polka regards everyday life phenomena, argues with cultural and design-specific situations and carries the ease of life forward on the way to create ‚product pleasures'.

www.polkaproducts.com

Tattoo

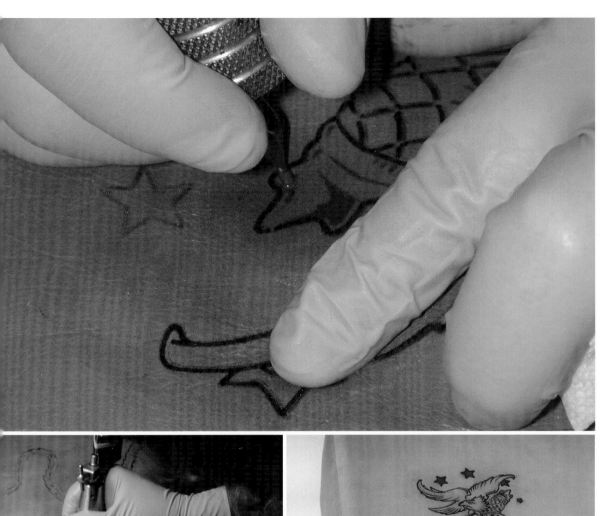

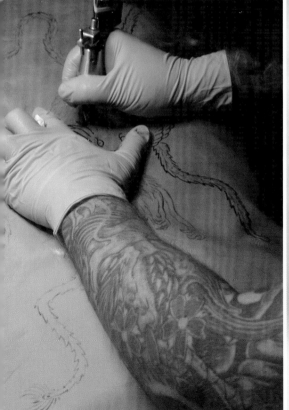

POOL22 | BERLIN, GERMANY

Frank Hesselmann, Murat Kocyigit

Pool22 is a young design company in Berlin. In their creations, you'll find an engagement with space and function connected with individual solutions, showing the small differences in everyday life.

www.pool22.de

1 Spieszer Kollektion
2 Gästezaun
3 Teller Trick

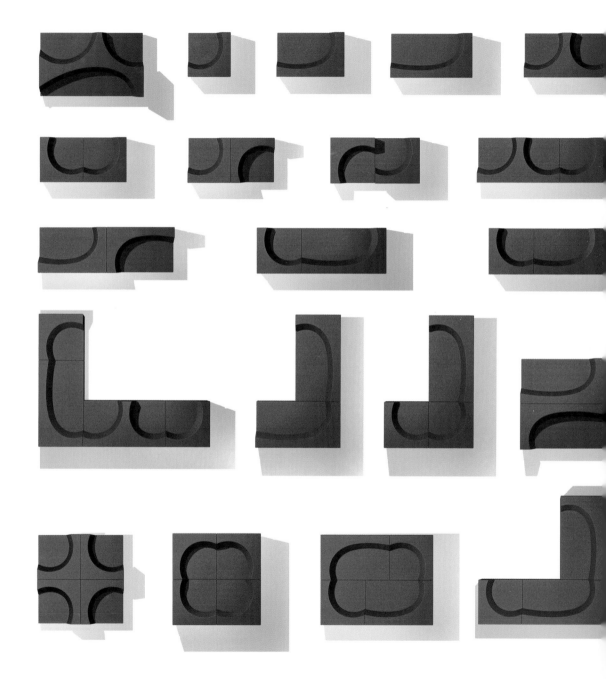

JACOB PRINGIERS DESIGN STUDIO I MILAN

Jacob Pringiers design studio is a young and dynamic creative resource operating in the most varied design markets.

www.jacobpringiers.com

1 Baia, *modular seating system*
2 Twice
3 Sonic (designed by Jacob Pringiers and Luca Casini)

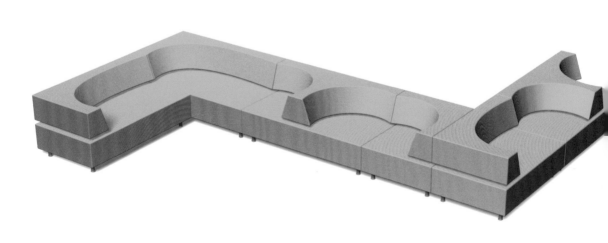

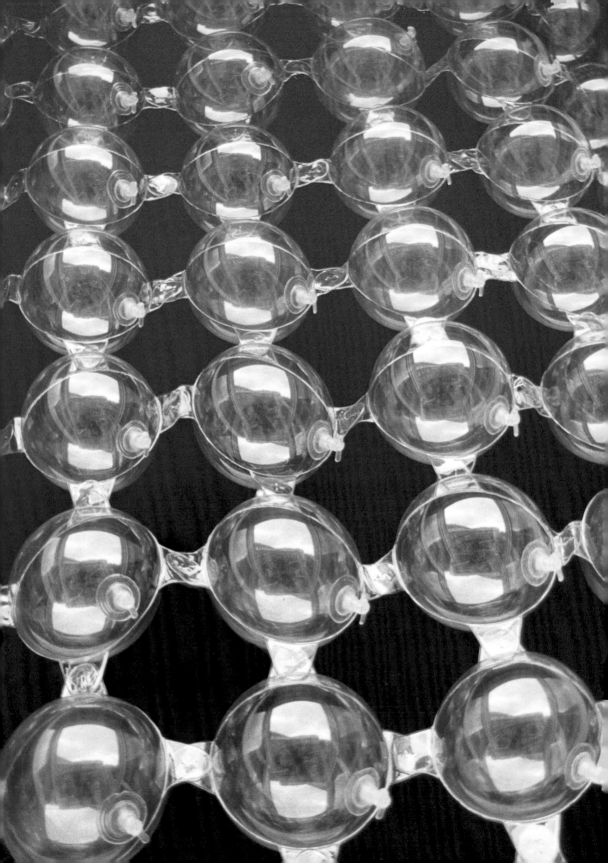

PUFF_BUFF DESIGN | WARSAW, POLAND
Anna Siedlecka, Radek Achramowicz

Immateriality and surprise. Lightweight objects and movable systems. Things that want to be touched, that bring enjoyment and beauty.

www.puff-buff.com

1 Bubbles, *inflated screen*
2 Blue Grass
3 led underwear cloth lamp
4 X_Wing
5 thunder interactiv lamp

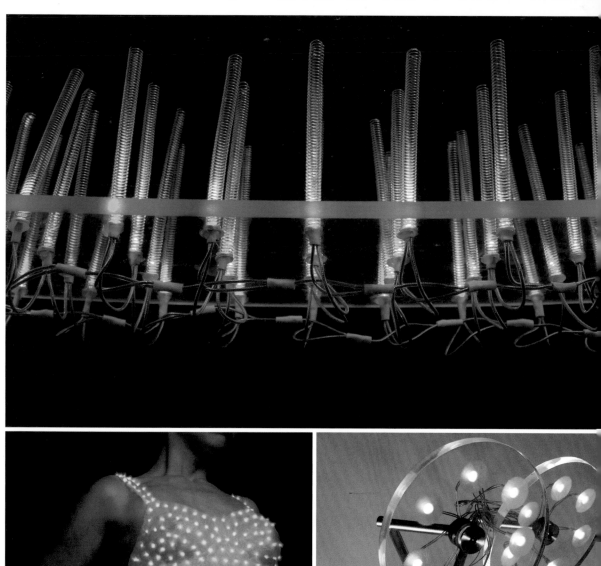

3

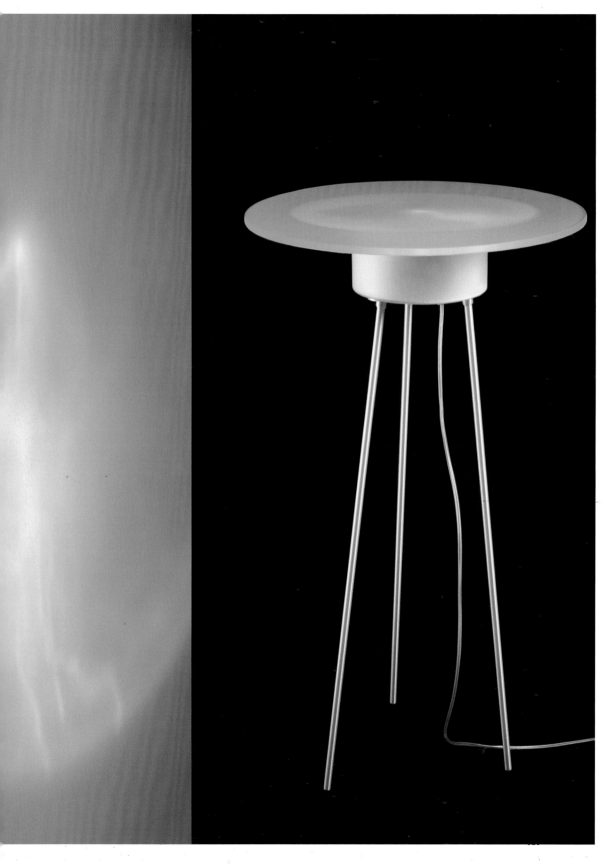

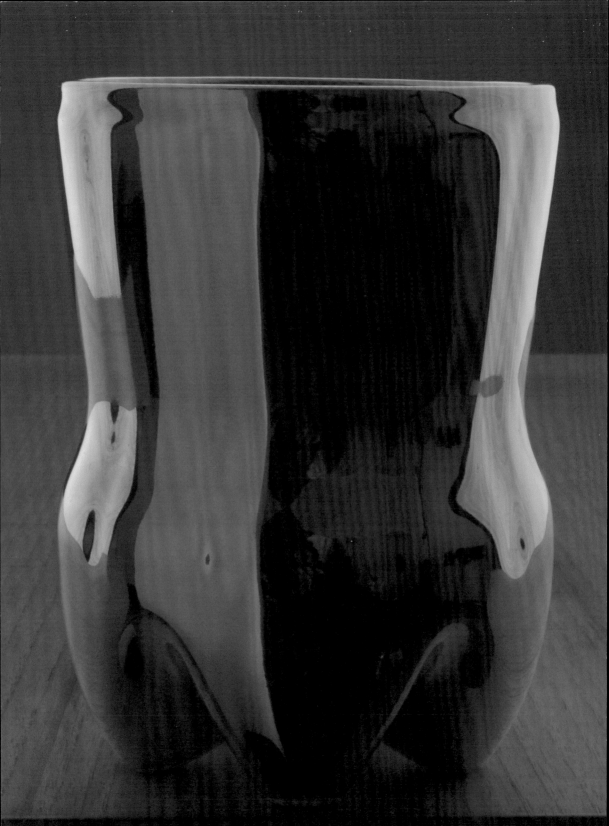

QUBUS DESIGN STUDIO | PRAGUE, CZECH REPUBLIC
Vladimira Kocicova

Studio Qubus have a background in sculpture. Their work ranges from one-off commission pieces to complete interior design projects and installations.

www.qubus.cz

Golden Edition

RANSMEIER & FLOYD DESIGN SERVICES | EINDHOVEN, THE NETHERLANDS
Leon Ransmeier, Gwen Floyd

The work of Ransmeier & Floyd holds great respect for the tenents of modernist design but believe that placing an emphasis on cultural and material communication can give modernism a greater contemporary sensibility.

www.ransmeierfloyd.com

1 D.I.Y.M (do it yourself modern)
2 Big date
3 Worn in
4 Gradient

SEBASTIAN RITZLER | **KIEL, GERMANY**
VINCENT HOLGER WECKERT | **MUNICH, GERMANY**

Not technology, but material or formalism is the origin of their projects. Combined the right way, they embody this approach.

s.ritzler@web.de
vincent_weckert@yahoo.com

Amun, *electric power visualisation*

SANNIADESIGN | **MILAN, ITALY**
Sam Sannia

Sam Sannia is a product and furniture designer. His philosophy: "when a project works, it's got no edges on it: it's a sphere and it rolls".

www.sanniadesign.com

1 Panca
2 Vallet
3 Geeza
4 Vaso

JOHN SEBASTIAN | COPENHAGEN, DENMARK

At an age of only 30, John Sebastian has designed everything from a coffee jug, lightning, furniture, a bathroom
collection, watches to a concept bycicle.

www.johnsebastian.dk

1 Watch
2 Easy chair collection
3 Glow, *a family of hand-blown glass lamps*
4 JS01 Biomega, *concept bike*

SPEZIELL PRODUKTGESTALTUNG | **OFFENBACH, GERMANY**
Sybille Fleckenstein, Jens Pohlmann, Thilo Schwer

speziell produktgestaltung design special products which exist
in the realm between the obvious and the unusual.

www.speziell.net

1 Tischlicht
2 Ringe
3 Tablett
4 Kommode

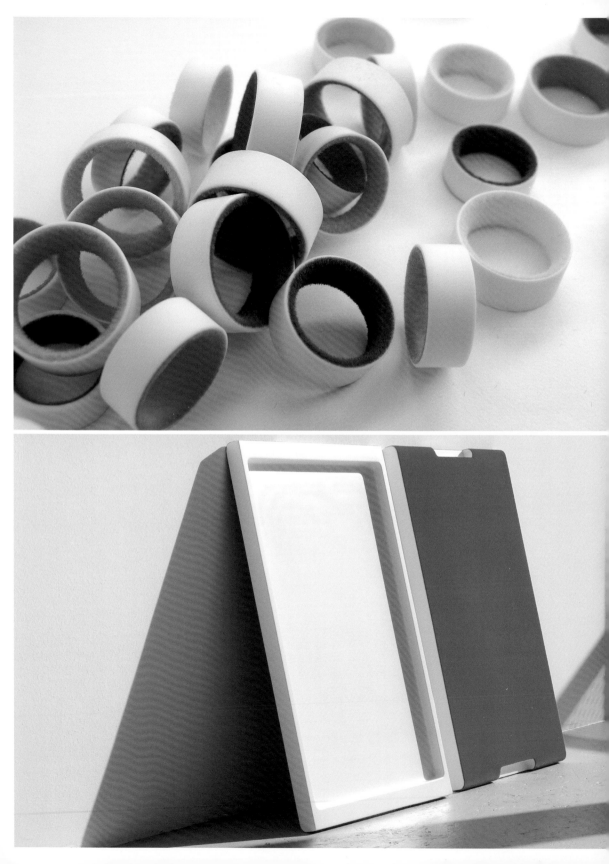

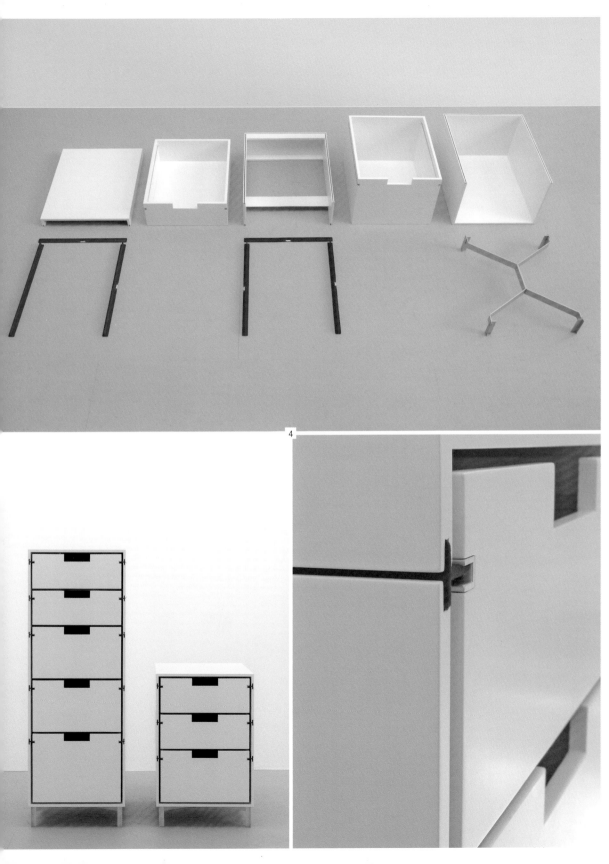

STERNFORM PRODUKTGESTALTUNG | ULM, GERMANY
Andrea Großfuss, Olaf Kießling

Sternform specialize in furniture, accessories and all kind
of products surrounding and concerning people

www.sternform.de

1 Anstifter, *notebookholder with pencil*
2 Drei-mal-Fünf, *shelf*
3 Twin, *thermos bowls*
4 Moerser, *mortar*
5 Niklas, *porcelain*
6 Babuschka, *chair*

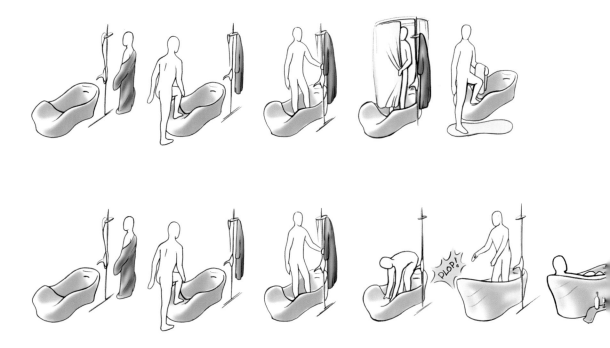

MARTIN STRUSS CREATIVE INDUSTRY | BRATISLAVA, SLOVAK REPUBLIC

Creative Industry combines product concept, design and visual identity, with a focus on usability.

www.creativeindustry.net

Kvapka, *bath concept*

STUDIO MÀSS | MALAKOFF, FRANCE
Olivier Chabaud, Laurent Lévêque

Amazingly contemporary, each Studio màss project stages the use of the object as an impulsion to its own narration. Each solution then stems from a personal deed, from a movement, from an intimate conversation.

www.mass.fr

1 chaise am:pm
2 Coupelle Nef
3 Carafe Ondine
4 Soliflore Flow
5 Transat epsilon
6 Tabouret hélium
7 Liz

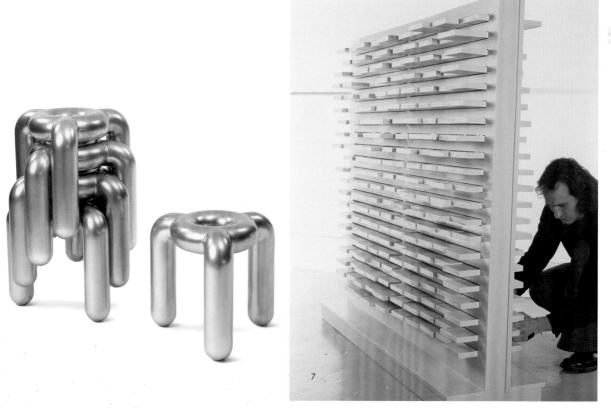

STUDIO VERTIJET | HALLE, GERMANY
Kirsten Antje Hoppert, Steffen Kroll

Kirsten Antje Hoppert and Steffen Kroll think universally and work generally – from the space station to book illustration – everything is interesting to them.

www.vertijet.de

1 Cutting Crew
2 Appetizer
3 Scroll
4 Gubmachobschi

2

RENE SULC INDUSTRIAL DESIGN | PRAGUE, CZECH REPUBLIC

Rene Sulc, a freelance designer, works as a lighting, furniture and industrial designer.

www.rene-sulc.com

1 Durink
2 Crutches
3 Chaise longue
4 T-Chair

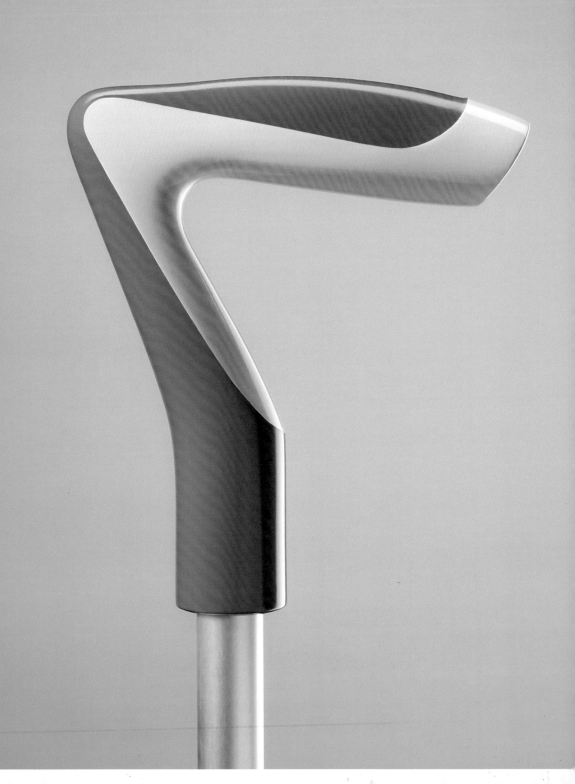

SUTER&GIL DISEÑO INDUSTRIAL | MADRID, SPAIN
Pascal Suter, Jaime Gil Narvarte

Suter&Gil is an industrial design studio created in 1997
that produces furniture, lighting and accessories for
European companies.

www.suterygil.com

1 Book
2 Spoon
3 Box
4 Tereo

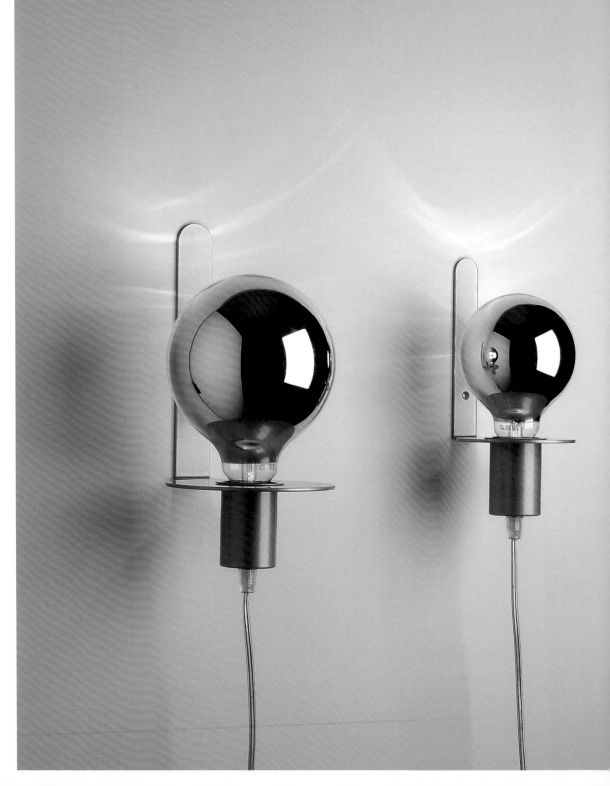

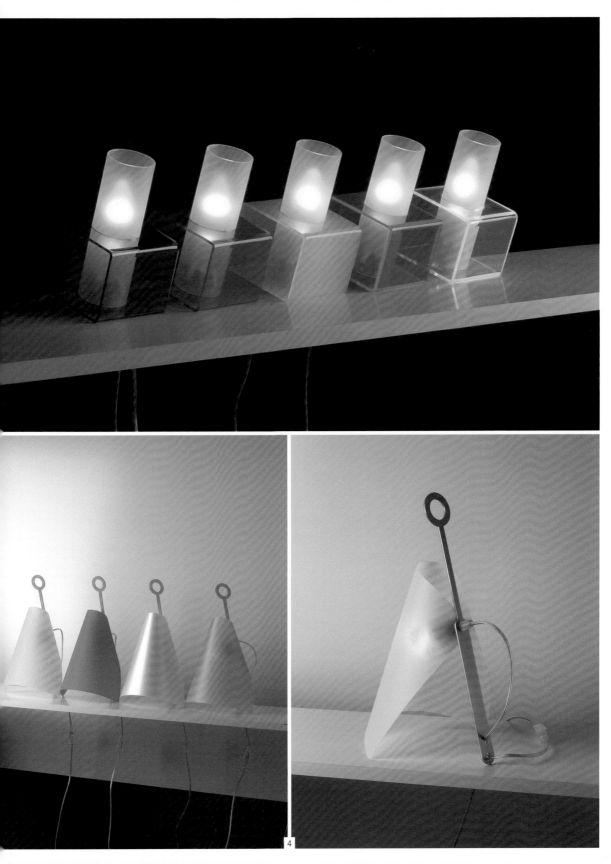

TAIONE | PRAGUE, CZECH REPUBLIC
Henry Wigus, Martin Hasek

Taione was founded in 2004 as a product and interior design studio. To start an discussion about new role of design, how to make good design inexpensive and accessible to wider public, make products cheaper and therefore more accessible substantiate her design claim.

www.taione.cz

1 Kedra.01
2 Pau Tau
3 Boxik.02
4 Party!

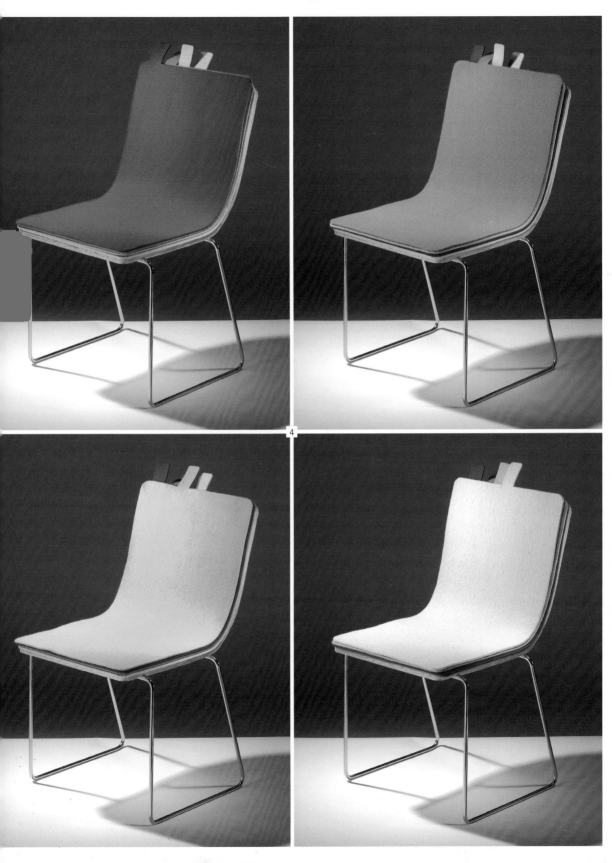

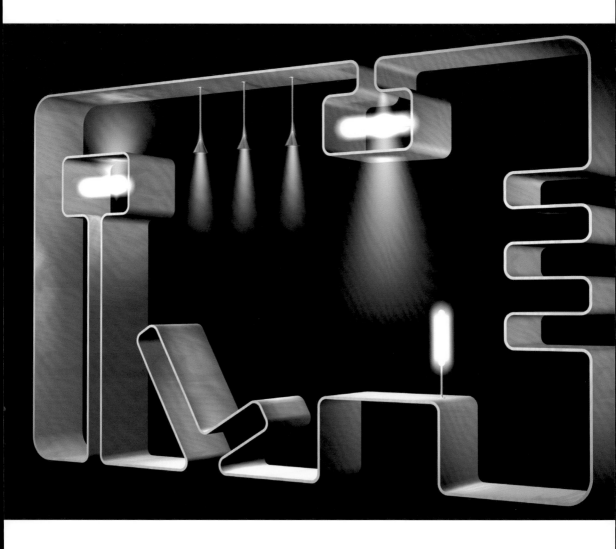

TRANSALPIN | MILAN, ITALY
Björn Blisse, Folker Königbauer, Reinhard Zetsche

Visions and experiments are the basis for innovative products. Then you can start strategic product development for success on the markets.

www.transalpin.net

1 Living in a box
2 Cubix
3 e-Wood

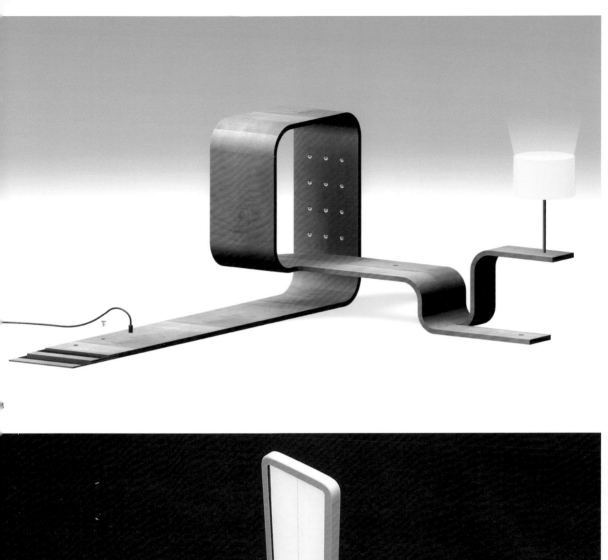
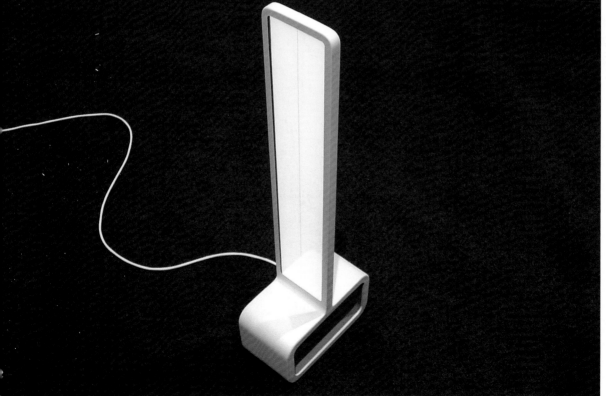

TIBOR UHRIN | **KOŠICE, SLOVAK REPUBLIC**

Independent designer and maker of furniture, stainless
steel and wooden dishes, vessels and tableware, toys, gift
objects and wooden percussion instruments.

www.uhrindesign.com

Table for Mr. Hale and Mr. Bopp and basket Zeppelin

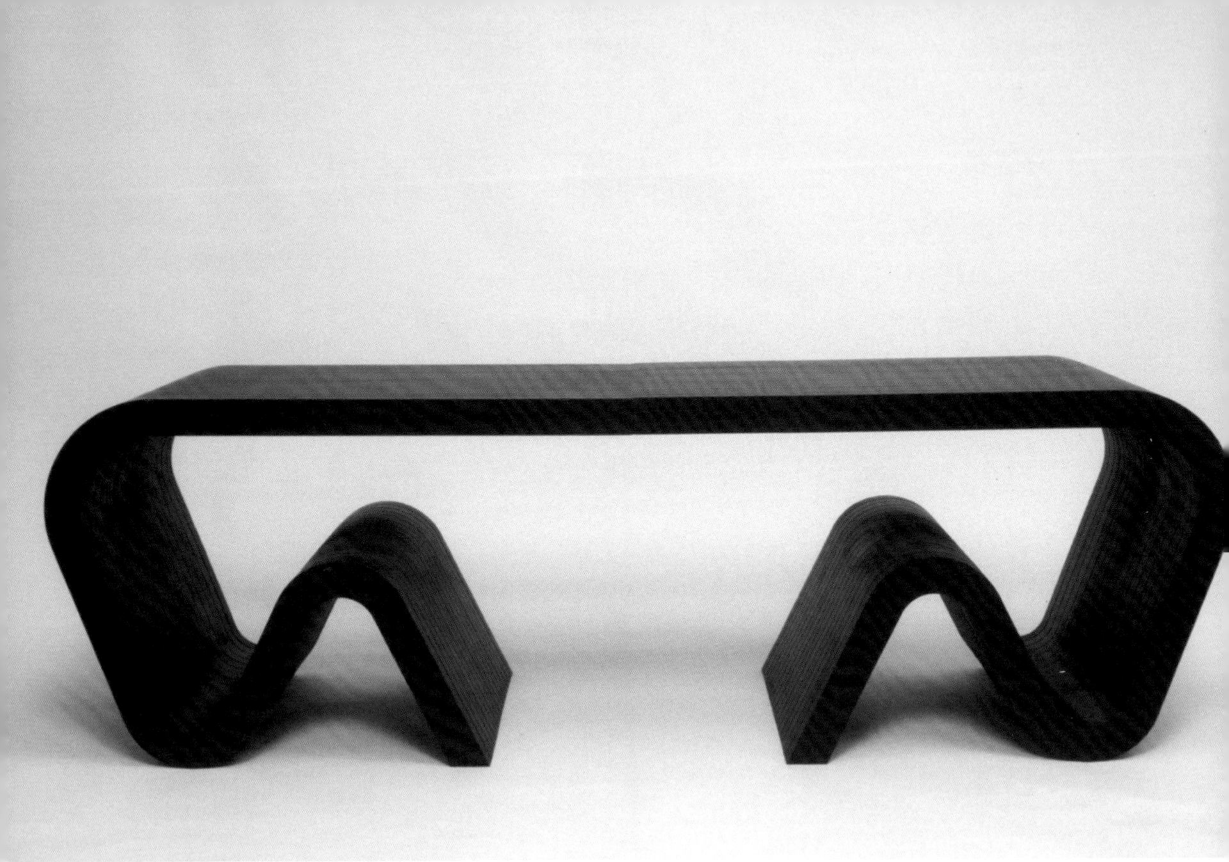

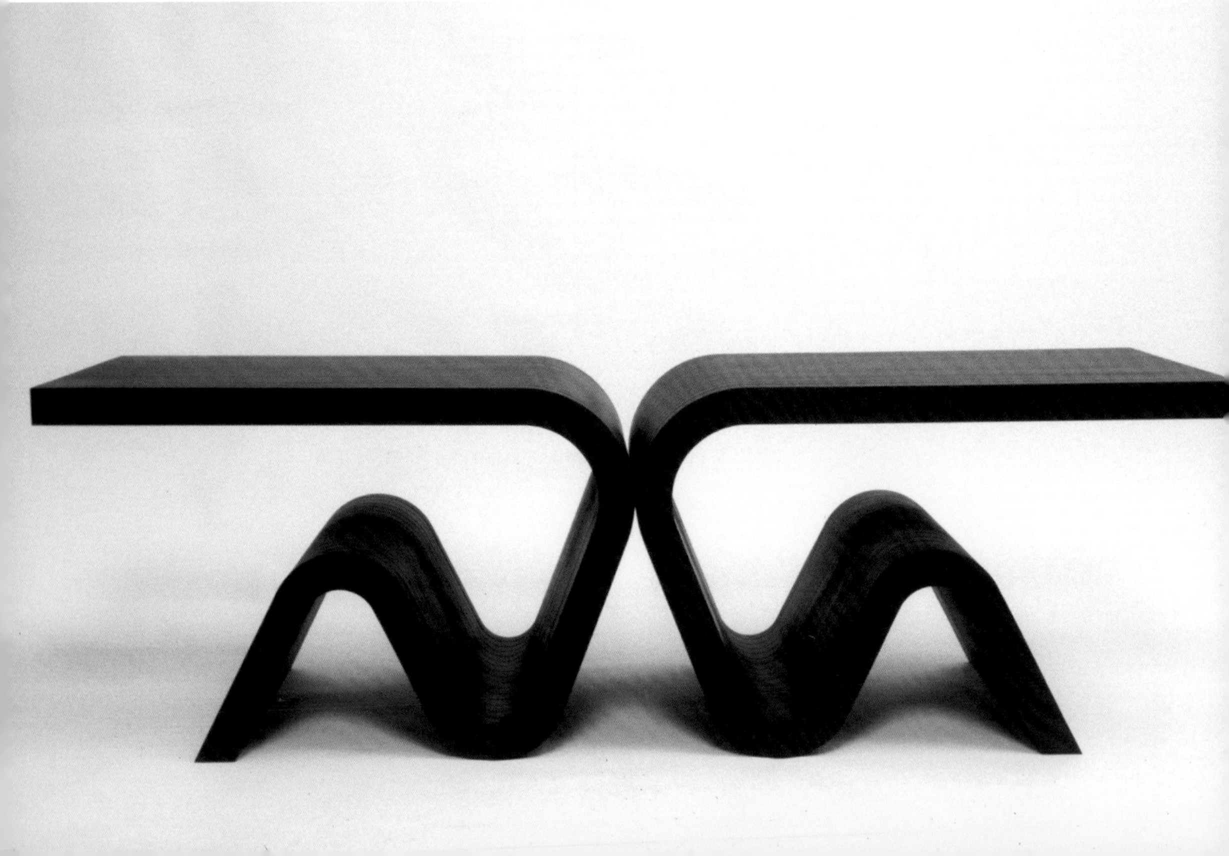

GARY VAN BROEKHOVEN | LONDON, UNITED KINGDOM

Gary van Broekhoven, an award-winning British designer, creates contemporary products with an emphasis on function, aesthetics and quality materials. His work challenges the boundaries between sculpture and product design.

www.gvb-uk.com

The Twins

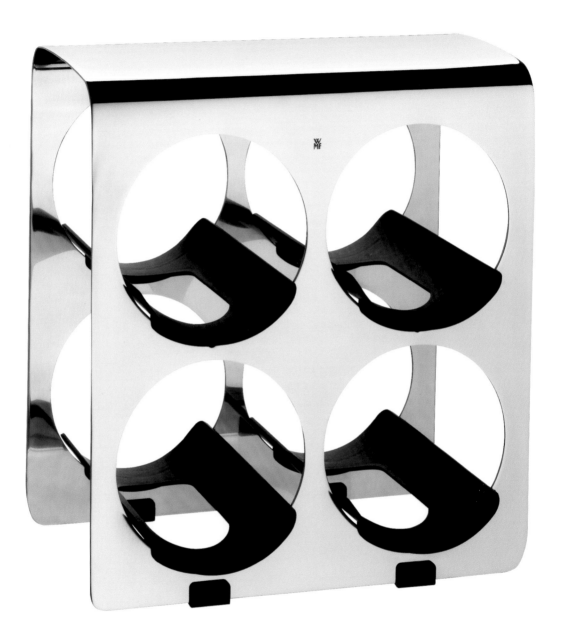

WOLF UDO WAGNER | **FRANKFURT, GERMANY**

For Wolf U. Wagner, the challenge in designing new products is to relate the context between humans, environment, culture and product: "I design the space between things".

www.wagner-design.de

1 Weinregal
2 "Luminale" (Leica Exhibition)
3 Culture Tableware
4 Lounger 02

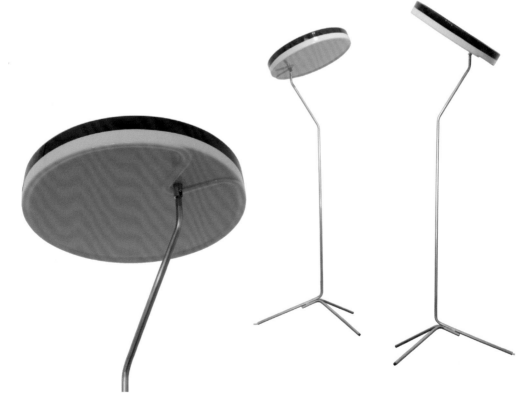

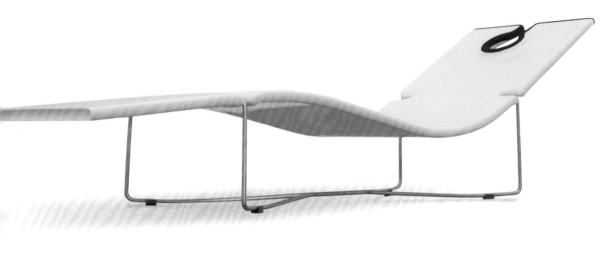

THEO WILLIAMS | AMSTERDAM, THE NETHERLANDS

Theo Williams has designed products for Alessi, Danese, Dornbracht, Mobileffe, Technogym, Giorgio Armani, and SKY. The bathroom collection 'Risma' for Merati was selected for the ADI Design Index 2003/4, Compasso d'Oro 2004, and awarded by the Wallpaper Design Awards.

www.theowilliams.com

1 Davos
2 Loure, *champagner glass*
3 Oyo, *USB multiplug*
4 Oyo, *telephone wire*

3

4

YUNIIC | ZURICH, SWITZERLAND

Thierry Villavieja, Christina Primschitz

Yuniic designs fresh furniture, objects and accessories with clear forms and a certain wink.

www.yuniic.ch

1 wing chair
2 sea.t.able
3 input
4 lucky
5 trophäe

3

4

5

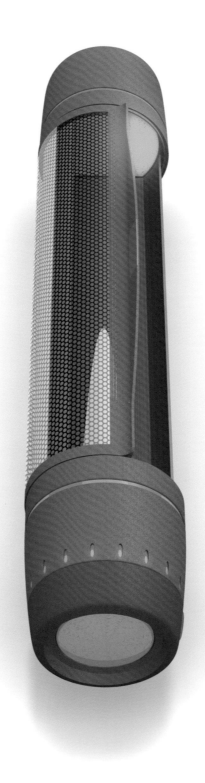

MARTIN ŽAMPACH | **UHERSKÝ BROD, CZECH REPUBLIC**

Style, reduction and social consideration are consistent themes throughout Martin Žampach's design work.

www.marti.cz

baggetty, *lamp*

INDEX

5.5 Designers | Paris   12
www.cinqcinqdesigners.com
Photos: Courtesy 5.5. Designers

Agence A+ Créateurs D'Objects | Paris   16
www.a-plus.fr
Photos: Courtesy Agence A+ Créateurs D'Objects

**Afroditi Krassa Industrial Design
Consultancy | London**   20
www.afroditi.com
Photos: Emma Mitchell, Afroditi Krassa

Ahn and Ahn Industrial Design | Como   24
www.ahnandahn.com
Photos: Courtesy Ahn and Ahn Industrial Design

ALL-Interieur | Geel   28
www.all-interieur.be
Photos: Stijn Schauwers

Julian Appelius Büro für Produkt Design | Berlin   32
www.julianappelius.de
Photos: Courtesy Julian Appelius

Studio Claudia Santiago Areal | Dachau   36
www.claudiasantiagoareal.de
Photos: Jona C. Heckl, Christoph Gramann

autoban | Galata   40
www.autoban212.com
Photos: Courtesy Autoban

Barber Osgerby | London   44
www.barberosgerby.com
Photos: Courtesy Barber Osgerby

Barney Barford | London   48
www.barneybarford.co.uk
Photos: Courtesy Barney Barford

**Alberto Basaglia Natalia Rota Nodari Architetti
Associatii | Bergamo**   52
www.ydf.it
Photos: Courtesy YDF Young Designers Factory

Paul Bechstein | Brackenheim   56
www.paulbechstein.com1
Photos: Courtesy Marcel Heinz

Gabriela Bellon Furniture Design | Frankfurt   60
www.gabrielabellon.com
Photos: Dejan Vekic

Bernstrand & Co | Stockholm   64
www.bernstrand.com
Photos: Zero AB, Pär Backstrand, Fredrik Sandin Carlson,
Bianca Pilet

Berteling Design | Notre Dame de l'Osier   68
www.berteling-design.com
Photos: Courtesy Berteling Design

**Michaël Bihain Interior &
Furniture design | Bruxelles**   70
www.michaelbihain.com
Photos: Courtesy Michaël Bihain

bkm Design Working Group | Vienna   74
www.bkm-format.com
Photos: Gerhard Ramsebner, Courtesy bkm

Bram Boo | St-Truiden   78
www.bramboo.be
Photos: Frank Gielen, Lieven Herreman, Hugo Maertens,
Wim Vanderstraeten

Todd Bracher Studio | Paris   82
http://go.to/toddbracher
Photos: Thomas Damgaard, Zanotta, Courtesy Todd Bracher
Studio

Buro Bruno | Arnhem   88
www.burobruno.nl
Photos: Courtesy Buro Bruno

Louise Campbell | Copenhagen   92
www.louisecampbell.com
Photos: Courtesy Louise Campbell

chd Industrial & Product Design | Athen   96
www.chd.gr
Photos: Courtesy chd Industrial & Product Design

CIPRE Design | Nice   100
www.cipre.fr
Photos: Courtesy Cipre Design

code.2.design | Stuttgart   104
www.code2design.de
Photos: Courtesy code.2.design

**confused collection konzeption und
gestaltung | Berlin**   108
www.confused-collection.de
Photos: Courtesy Confused Collection

CROSS|CREATIVE Designstudios | Pforzheim   112
www.crosscreative.de
Photos: Alexander Grüber, Flashpoint Studio

daniels & koitzsch Designer | Darmstadt   118
www.daniels-koitzsch.de
Photos: Courtesy Micha Daniels, Stefan Koitzsch

Cédric Debatty | Flémalle   120
cedricdebatty@skynet.bz
Photos: Courtesy Cédric Debatty

Maria de Ros | Barcelona   122
mariaderos@hotmail.com
Photos: Courtesy Maria de Ros

defacto.design | Munich 126
www.defactodesign.de
Photos: Mierswa & Kluska

dejanew | Prague 130
www.dejanew.cz
Photos: Courtesy dejanew

Delineo Design | Montebelluna 132
www.delineodesign.it
Photos: Andrea Pancino, Carlo Bazan, Antonio Cervi

Design Aid | Prague 136
dariapodboj@centrum.cz
Photos: Daria Podboj

Design by us | Copenhagen 138
www.design-by-us.com
Photos: Mikkel Strange

Lilian de Souza | Karlsruhe 142
www.liliandesouza.net
Photos: Martin Morlock

Stephanie Dietmann | Frankfurt 144
stephanie.dietmann@gmx.net
Photos: Vera Siegmund

Stefan Diez | Munich 146
www.stefan-diez.com
Photos: Courtesy Stefan Diez

Disorder Collectiv | Kortrijk 152
www.disorder.be
Photos: Courtesy Disorder Collectiv

element Design | Vienna 156
www.element.co.at
Photos: Courtesy element Design

Fashionsteel Möbeldesign | Basel 160
www.fashionsteel.ch
Photos: Courtesy Fashionsteel Möbeldesign

feinedinge handmade
produktgestaltung | Vienna 162
www.feinedinge.at
Photos: Sandra Haischberger, Daniela Beranek

Fifty-Eight b | Dublin 166
www.fiftyeightb.ie
Photos: Courtesy Fifty-Eight b

File studio | Prague 170
www.file-studio.com
Photos: Courtesy File Studio

For Use | Vienna 174
foruse@eunet.at
Photos: Marino Ramazzotti, Studio Controluce,
Courtesy For Use

Freedom Of Creation | Amsterdam 178
www.freedomofcreation.com
Photos: Courtesy Freedom Of Creation

Fremdkörper | Cologne 180
www.solutionsfornoproblem.com
Photos: Falko Wenzel

Front | Stockholm 182
www.frontdesign.se
Photos: Katja Kristoferson, Anna Lönnerstam

Jörg Gätjens Design Development | Cologne 188
www.joerg-gaetjens.com
Photos: Courtesy Jörg Gätjens

Godart Designers | Paris 192
godart.designers@aol.com
Photos: Domingo Djuric

Camilla Groth | Helsinki 194
camillagroth@hotmail.com
Photos: Courtesy Camilla Groth

gruppe RE | Cologne 198
www.gruppe-re.de
Photos: Kessler Communications, Lukas Roth,
Courtesy gruppe RE

Doug Harper Furniture | London 202
www.hiddenart.com
Photos: Stephen Brayne

Hippos Design Architektura | Prague 204
www.hipposdesign.com
Photos: Courtesy Hippos Design Architektura,
Filip Slapal, Adam Holy

iL-studio | Amsterdam 208
www.il-studio.nl
Photos: Courtesy iL-Studio

instantconcept buero für gestaltung, design,
innenarchitektur | Wuppertal 212
www.instantconcept.com
Photos: Gunnar Bäldle, Tim Nottebaum

irion Möbelsysteme | Winterthur 216
www.irion.li
Photos: Christian Amman

Florence Jaffrain | Paris 218
www.moaproduction.com
Photos: Courtesy Florence Jaffrain

jehs + laub | Stuttgart 222
www.jehs-laub.de
Photos: Courtesy jehs + laub

kafka.design | Berlin 226
www.kafkadesign.de
Photos: Nico Hesselmann, Henk John, Marc Räder

Studio Monni Karri | Helsinki 230
www.lapalma.it
Photos: Courtesy Lapalma

Kik! | Eindhoven 234
www.kikiworld.nl
Photos: Courtesy Kik!

Michael Koenig | Hamburg 236
www.studiomichaelkoenig.com
Photos: André Reinke, Markus Heumann

Lifestyle Space | London 240
www.theoculas.com
Photos: Lee McCormack

Patrick Lindon | Oberwil bei Zug 242
www.patrick-lindon.com
Photos: Courtesy Patrick Lindon

Lorenz Kaz | Milano 246
www.lorenz-kaz.com
Photos: Courtesy Lorenz Kaz

Felix Severin Mack | Esslingen 248
www.felix-severin-mack.com
Photos: Markus S. H. Hänchen, Darius Ramazani

maybe design | Istanbul 252
www.maybedesign.at
Photos: Courtesy maybe Design

Julia Maendler Designer | Paris 256
pixxpaxx@hotmail.com
Photos: Kali Vermes

Manzlab | Copenhagen 258
www.manzlab.dk
Photos: Erik Brahl, Frederica Furniture

design by f maurer | Vienna 262
www.fmaurer.com
Photos: Franz Helmreich

momentum | Zurich 266
www.momentumdesign.ch
Photos: Courtesy momentum

monica graffeo designer | Zoppola di Pordenone 270
www.monicagraffeo.it
Photos: Courtesy Monica Graffeo

Roberto Monte | Pagani 274
www.m2design.it
Photos: Gaetano Del Mauro

Walter Musacchi | Berlin 276
www.waltermusacchi.com
Photos: Courtesy Walter Musacchi

Thorsten Neeland | London 278
www.torsten-neeland.co.uk
Photos: WMF, Anthologie Quartett, Auerhahn, Dornbracht, Metz/Racine

Neustahl | Luzern 282
www.neustahl.ch
Photos: Courtesy Neustahl

Nichetto+Gai | Venezia 284
www.spunklab.it
Photos: Salviati, Stefano Medda, Luca Nichetto

Nix | London 290
www.annettenix.com
Photos: Courtesy Annette Nix

Olze & Wilkens | Berlin 292
www.olzewilkens.de
Photos: Courtesy Olze & Wilkens

Dieter Paul Design | Graz 296
www.dipaul.com
Photos: Courtesy Dieter Paul

Pearsonlloyd Design | London 300
www.pearsonlloyd.co.uk
Photos: Courtesy Pearsonlloyd Design

Florian Petri | Berlin 304
www.fpid.de
Photos: Courtesy Florian Petri

The Pfeifer Consultancy | London 306
www.leonhardpfeifer.com
Photos: Chris King, Courtesy Leonard Pfeifer

Polka Product Pleasure | Vienna 310
www.polkaproducts.com
Photos: Courtesy Polka Product Pleasure

POOL22 | Berlin 314
www.pool22.de
Photos: Courtesy Pool22

jacob pringiers design studio | Milano 318
www.jacobpringiers.com
Photos: BRF, Desalto, WMF

puff_buff design | Warsaw 322
www.puff-buff.com
Photos: Courtesy puff_buff design

Qubus Design Studio | Prague 326
www.qubus.cz
Photos: Marek Novotný

Ransmeier&Floyd | Eindhoven 328
www.ransmeierfloyd.com
Photos: Courtesy Ransmeier&Floyd

Sebastian Ritzler I Kiel   332
s.ritzler@web.de
Photos: Peter Riering-Czekalla

Peter Riering-Czekalla I San Francisco   332
peter@riering-czekalla.de
Photos: Courtesy Peter Riering-Czekalla

sanniadesign I Milano   334
www.sanniadesign.com
Photos: Matteo Mezzalira, Courtesy Sanniadesign

John Sebastian I Copenhagen   338
www.johnsebastian.dk
Photos: Courtesy John Sebastian

speziell produktgestaltung I Offenbach   342
www.speziell.net
Photos: Courtesy speziell produktgestaltung

Sternform Produktgestaltung I Ulm   346
www.sternform.de
Photos: Courtesy Sternform Produktgestaltung

Martin Struss Creative Industry I Bratislava   352
www.creativeindustry.net
Photos: Courtesy Martin Struss Creative Industry

Studio màss I Malakof   354
www.mass.fr
Photos: Courtesy Studio màss

studio vertijet I Halle   358
www.vertijet.de
Photos: Courtesy studio vertijet

Rene Sulc Industrial Design I Prague   362
www.rene-sulc.com
Photos: Petra Hajska, Petr Karsulin,
3. Frantisek Chrastek, Filip Slapal

Suter & Gil I Madrid   366
www.suterygil.com
Photos: Courtesy Suter & Gil

Taione Design I Prague   370
www.taione.cz
Photos: Courtesy Taione Design

Transalpin I Milan   374
www.transalpin.net
Photos: Courtesy Transalpin

Tibor Uhrin I Košice   378
www.uhrindesign.com
Photos: Dusan Slivka

Gary van Broekhoven I London   380
www.gvb-uk.com
Photos: Courtesy Gary van Broekhoven

Wolf Udo Wagner I Frankfurt   382
www.wagner-design.de
Photos: Courtesy Wolf Udo Wagner

Vincent Holger Weckert I Munich   332
vincent_weckert@yahoo.com
Photos: Peter Riering-Czekalla

Theo Williams I Amsterdam   386
www.theowilliams.com
Photos: Carlo Lavatori

yunniic I Zurich   390
www.yuniic.ch
Photos: Courtesy yuniic, Sandra Hanak

Martin Žampach | Uhersky Brod   394
www.marti.cz
Photos: Courtesy Martin Žampach

© 2005 daab
cologne   london   new york

published and distributed worldwide by
daab gmbh
friesenstr. 50
d - 50670 köln

p   +49-221-94 10 740
f   +49-221-94 10 741

mail@daab-online.de
www.daab-online.de

publisher ralf daab
rdaab@daab-online.de

art director feyyaz
mail@feyyaz.com

editor joachim fischer
fischer@brand-affairs.de

editorial project by fusion publishing gmbh stuttgart . los angeles
editorial direction martin nicholas kunz
© 2005 fusion publishing, www.fusion-publishing.com

layout kerstin graf, papierform
imaging jan hausberg

© frontcover olze & wilkens, © backcover dieter paul
© introduction photos page 7: gerhard ramsebner, page 9: barber osgerby, page 11: neustahl

introduction joachim fischer
english translation asco international, barbara sandre
french translation asco international, gérard cohen
spanish translation asco international, guillermo buchholz
italian translation asco international, bruna d'elia

printed in spain
gràfiques ibèria, spain
www.grupgisa.com

isbn 3-937718-42-7
d.l.: B-36444-2005